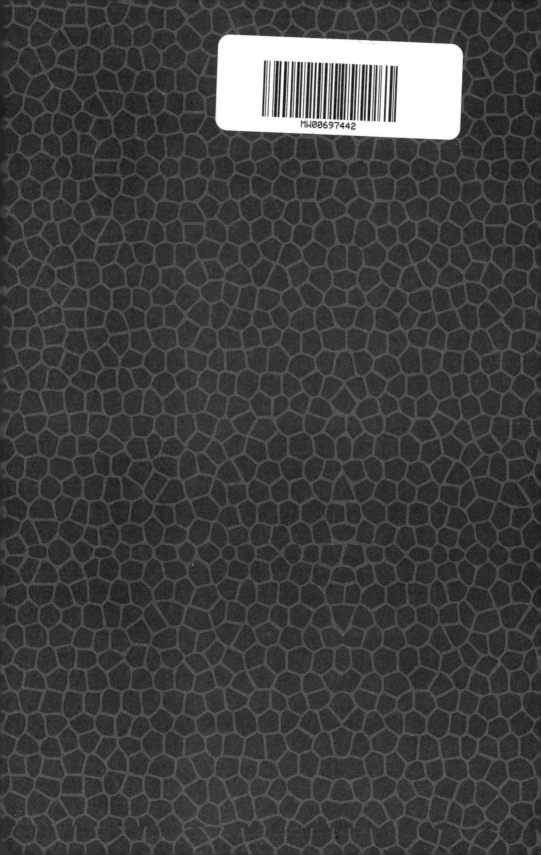

the
lamplighter

MOSAICA PRESS

ESTHER FEINSTEIN

the
lamplighter

EXPERIENCES OF A CHABAD REBBETZIN

Published by Mosaica Press, Inc.
www.mosaicapress.com
info@mosaicapress.com

Dedicated to

my father-in-law

whose patient ear, literary style,
and giving nature
brought this work to fruition

table of contents

acknowledgments

the Rebbe: It is your positivity bias to life that after all these years still encourages me. You always inspired and continue to inspire me. If I just read a small story about you each day or watch one of your interactions with people standing in line, then that is enough to get me through a tough day, and sometimes to flip it around to a brighter day.

The Rebbetzin: A true *rebbetzin* who was always behind the scenes yet turned over the world in such an incredible way. The stories that we always hear of her are about her strength and love for each person, big and small. I remember hearing a powerful story about the Rebbetzin. Someone once asked the Lubavitcher Rebbe, "What was the Rebbetzin to you?" He looked at the man and said, "She was my *pnimi* [my innermost self]." Even so many years after her passing, we are still getting to know her. What an incredible person, true role model, and leader she was.

To my better half and my partner in all things in life: I remember when I asked you if I could share our personal stories with our friends, in-laws, congregants, and even publish some on the *Times of Israel*. Each time I asked, for you it wasn't even a question. You always stand behind me on each step that I take to better myself and share with the world. Thank you!

To my amazing children: It was such an honor to sit and read with you many of these stories. You watched it all happen, and your support always touches my heart. How often would you sit on my lap and say, "Mommy, please read me a story." As I went to get a book you said, "No, one of your stories, please, Mommy!"

Heather Benson: To a special person who always—even during your midterms as the lecturer at a university—found time each week or whenever I needed you; you were always there. You have such a talent to not only edit my work but work alongside me and help me keep my unique style of writing. Thank you for being such a good friend and a wonderful person. I remember when I was nervous to even read you one of my stories. After each *Tanya* class, you asked gently if I have any stories for you, and I bashfully answered yes. You would encourage me to find my voice in each of these memoirs and reflections and bring it to life.

To my dear father-in-law: Thank you so much for believing in me. I remember each summer when the boys and I stayed in Chicago for summer camp, and I started writing in my diary. Each time I wrote a new story, you always listened to it even when you had the longest shift at the hospital. You always gave me the time of day and believed my stories were going to go somewhere.

To my most wonderful mother-in-law: It has been fifteen years of your support and kindness through thick and thin. You are such an incredible person. I loved sharing my stories with you. Thank you!

Rivka: I appreciate you so much for taking the time to help me with this project. Your schedule is so hectic, and yet you always were there helping me along the way.

Rabbi Chaim Miller: Thank you so much for everything. I remember when I had the chutzpah to call you. You were such a mensch and you helped me brainstorm many different ideas. It was such an awesome experience. You showed me how even famous incredible authors can reach out to one's fellow and help them.

introduction

When I was around eight years old, the Lubavitcher Rebbe passed away, and all our lives in Chabad became very different. My memories of a packed 770 Eastern Parkway, black hats bouncing to songs of the heart, and standing in line for hours to receive dollars, had all stopped. One might wonder, why stand in line for hours? Was it just for a single dollar?

The idea of receiving a dollar was to partner with the Lubavitcher Rebbe in doing the *mitzvah* (commandment) of giving charity. However, to me and most others, the idea one stood in line for was just to hear a whisper, see a signal, or receive a smile, and that let you know that you were special to him. I remember when my turn came in line: the Rebbe smiled at me; my whole world stopped, and I floated home.

After Gimmel Tammuz, the date honored for the Rebbe's passing, I thought it would be the end of Chabad and the movement. Going out to help others would become a thing of the past. In retrospect, it was just beginning to build in its momentum, and many more Chabad houses (over five thousand today) sprung up even in the most dangerous of places—just to help other people. The Rebbe taught one to embrace positivity in each step that he led.

Many looking from the outside wondered how we could continue without a Rebbe. How could that be? What would we do? However, the strength came from within each and every one of us not to forget what the Lubavitcher Rebbe stood for and what his dreams were. It is us, embracing his vision of light for the world, that keeps us warm even in the darkest of times. Reading and remembering his words brings us a real understanding of *"k'ish echad b'lev echad"* (our being one people united in our hearts) and the *mitzvah* of *"v'ahavta l'reiacha k'mocha"* (loving your fellow as yourself).

1

After the Holocaust, the Jewish people were broken as a nation, and the Rebbe helped to pick up the pieces and showed us as a people how to create a world of positivity and peace. The Rebbe built an army of his emissaries—or "his children," as he termed us—and our mission is to uplift each fallen person and let them know he or she is not alone.

I began writing this book over seven years ago. I was going through a deep personal tragedy, and I felt the need to have a diary again. I used to have a diary as a little girl, as did most little girls when I was growing up. It was this club that we had amongst close friends, and it was a way to communicate with one another, a way to feel special, and a chance to reflect on the day's events regardless as to whether there was any momentary drama or not.

I started to write about "my secret *shlichus* life" in the tiny office that we had. I wrote when my children were deep asleep, tired out from our long, packed days. I choose this life no matter how challenging or difficult my position or outpost as an emissary became. I choose to be a Chabad emissary, and this means that my life is no longer my own. My life is meant for others, and it will never be truly mine, and this is what gave me a sense of peace and what I fought for: to be a pillar for my community, family, and the world.

The Lubavitcher Rebbe was unique in his role of uplifting Jewish women way before the time when this approach became popular. One can wonder: What is the beauty of a Jewish woman? What is our role supposed to be? This always seems to be the women's struggle within, wondering where we belong. In today's world, women are expected to live in a man's world and to try to be more like a man.

However, the way to truly see the job of the Jewish woman is by doing what the Rebbe told and showed us. He always explained that the Jewish woman is the pillar and foundation of the home. When we look at humankind, we should look at men, women, and children as a family unit, rather than dividing them into categories.

The Rebbe always took his lead from his wife, Rebbetzin Chaya Mushka Schneerson. She was also the daughter of the previous Lubavitcher Rebbe, and she led by example how a Jewish woman should be. She always raised the bar for herself on *tikun olam* (making the world a better place), and did not forget the great *mitzvah* of "*kol kevudah bas melech pinimah*," the idea meaning, as one in Chabad would translate, that "the beauty of the king's daughter is within," a reference to the Rebbetzin's modesty in dress and character.

After I got married, I went from being a daughter of emissaries to being an emissary myself. There is nothing that truly prepares you for this type of job. I remember as a little eight-year-old girl that it was my dream to be an emissary and build a community.

It was this idea that many of the "Rebbe's children" had decided to give as a tribute to the Lubavitcher Rebbe. They then followed the dream of helping each person in need from all corners of the earth and hoping this great mission would bring about the redemption. It sounded like a silly idea to many, and many wondered if this could be a reality for us personally, but the dream stuck, and we as a couple went out on *shlichus*.

Being newlyweds with a baby on the way, life was already quite busy, but an emissary position came up, and we felt blessed to be able to go out immediately. This new position had stirred excitement within us, and we felt honored to fulfill our dreams of being *shluchim* (emissaries). We went to serve a large Russian Jewish community, even though it was in a very established place and nothing like my vision as a little girl—but it was ours. We had this incredible feeling that everything we touched grew wings as our hearts did. We breathed new life into each person we embraced. We rolled up our sleeves, and we felt content with the little and big things that fell into our laps.

It didn't matter that my husband's speeches were all in modern Hebrew or Russian; to me—regardless of the fact that these foreign words flew over and past me—this experience was a true fulfillment of what it means to be an emissary.

Circumstances led us to believe that the place was not for us, and the community would be better suited for a different couple. We decided that we had to move on, and our hearts were crushed. My head felt clouded, like feathers surrounded it with ideas, but nothing stuck, and our chance to go to a new position again seemed close to non-existent.

My husband and I felt broken for a time but vowed to go out once more. Hashem (G-d) heard our pleas, and we were granted our true destiny. We were honored that my husband's wish turned into a reality: the Rebbe sent us his emissary, the head *shliach*, to our living room. We were sent out to the Midwest, but this time, we did not have the privilege of having any preexisting religious infrastructure. There was no *mikvah* (bath for spiritual purity), no school for our children, no kosher food, and no proper shul. Everything would have to be built from scratch, and our lives became busy very fast.

Overnight, decisions that I used to have to contemplate for days or years needed to be made and turned into reality at a warp-speed rhythm.

We, as a family, could only find a small rented ranch home in which to organize our lives. After a short time living there, I told my husband that we had to give our home to the community, so members had a place to feel that was theirs, so we moved into a five-hundred-square-foot apartment. It didn't matter how emotionally difficult this move would be for us as a couple and a family: our *shlichus* needed to blossom. Our community needed us as spiritual parents, and everything else had to work itself out.

The long nights we spent working kept us apart and were hard, but the icy streets we had to walk each Friday night—from our tiny apartment to our first Chabad house—seemed like an impossibility. Somehow, it was the "not knowing" that made us determined as ever. In our "Frozen Tundra" city, would we be able to walk there each Friday night?

These questions pulled at us, but somehow it was like magic, and we made it each time—even with our little children slipping and sliding along a non-existent path. Our thoughts of "we can't do this" were ignored continuously, and only orchards of positivity did we allow ourselves to plant.

I used to be the girl who went to bed at 10:00 p.m.—and that was late for me! But on *shlichus*, at our post, we were like doctors on call, with each person in need setting our schedule. I am up super early, usually around 6:00 a.m., and go to bed super late, usually after 1:00 a.m., and that is the only way we, as emissaries, can finish everything at our post each day.

We go to bed knowing there is a pile-up of things that never ends. We keep moving despite our tired, aching limbs, and we keep pushing no matter how impossible things seem, for it is the only way to help a community with everything they need.

My husband and I on *shlichus* help out, as most rabbis and *rebbetzins* do within their communities. One's emotional, mental, and spiritual needs stay the same, but the last component is our main focus. We also help those in need financially (even when we barely have anything ourselves), and our phones never turn off.

It is a known thing amongst fellow emissaries that one should never leave his or her post. That means no vacation, or sabbatical year, or temporary *shlichus*. It is forever, and one can never retire, because emissaries are supposed to go down like a general in war: one has to stay dedicated to their spiritual children to the end.

It is inside this close circle that emissaries experience a tight brotherhood and sisterhood. However, everything else, at least to begin with, feels like one has been dropped off from New York and left—still with their suitcases—in the middle of nowhere. We made this drastic uproot from our cocooned Jewish neighborhood, our shtetl in New York, all to embrace our forgotten fellows in need. It becomes this new excitement, recognizing the importance of each Jew, that gives us the energy to survive this drastic lifestyle change that we imposed upon ourselves.

As a shy Brooklyn girl who was used to others giving their voice and was comfortable simply being a listener in the crowd, I now had no choice but to take center stage. At every turn and at each place my feet stand, people ask me for advice on what they should do. People in my community are always asking me for blessings and success in their day-to-day living, and I think to myself, "Me, give advice, or give a blessing? How can I help?"

Yet, as I grew into my role as a leader, *rebbetzin*, and mother to my community, my ability to give answers to the questions I am asked flows freer than it used to. After thirteen years of serving as an emissary, I forget to care about my shy self and just give as much as I can regardless of the fact that I have to force myself to walk outside my introverted shell. When someone is in need, I run!

Sometimes, there are even more difficult situations we must get involved in as emissaries. When it comes to couples and families, we take an active role in counseling. It can take a full day to work with couples and do marriage counseling between couples, and the phone never sleeps.

It is said that when Aharon HaKohen passed away, the whole nation mourned because he was busy with bringing *shalom bayis* (peace between couples) to families, and it was he, more than Moshe, that the community mourned. Aharon HaKohen's example shows how it is well worth it to put those long hours in.

However, the most challenging job wasn't figuring out how to procure kosher food, navigating how to reach the *mikvah* during snowstorms, or even doing the tedious job of teaching our own children. In fact, I actually fell in love with teaching my children and couldn't imagine life any other way. However, the hardest job was taking care of the great *mitzvah* of purifying the dead.

I remember when I was being groomed to take over the *chevra kadisha*, (burial society), and I didn't even realize that the group was training me to take over. No one told me their secret plan. This was because all the decisions were made behind closed doors, and a job usually given to the elders of the community was draped over my shoulders.

It was a job no one asked for, and no one could refuse when chosen. It could only be in our far-out "Frozen Tundra" where all Jews embrace each other regardless of title and difference of opinions. Who would believe that a Conservative shul, once Orthodox, would simply hand me the reins to their burial society, but hand me the reins they did. They had no choice but to pray that I would do the job and perform the tasks that the elders once did.

I asked this nice old Jewish man who headed the burial society, "How do you do it?" It was a sunny day, but the day seemed stormy and unbearable to me, because I was broken, and hurting inside at the thought of having to bury my friend's very young only daughter. I gripped the fence between us and asked him, "Does it get any easier?"

His wise old eyes stared at my nervous ones, and he said, "Yes, it does. It will happen when your focus is set straight, and it will no longer be about you, but about another in need. I buried my friends too, and have been alone in this job for many years. Sometimes, I am lucky to have a helper, but that is rare."

As I heard his words, I imagined to myself that I would never be alone and would never bury my friends. This old man soon was honored with my husband as his helper, and then shortly afterward, this great old man passed away.

A few years later, his words haunted me and then clung closer to me like an unsettling static. My nerves and worries followed me like a premonition of what was to come. I saw the foreshadowing, but destiny and fate would have it no other way, and I came to bury my friend and teacher.

A short time afterwards, I had to help a person who passed away and fulfill the *mitzvah* alone. It was the hardest thing I ever had to do, but like the kind old man told me, with time, I grew used to it. At times, when I have a helper, it feels wonderful, but whatever the situation, the quiet walls in a place of helping others shoo the worries away.

This is the life of an emissary. The job chooses us, and it makes us better people because of it. It means digging deeper inside oneself and pushing oneself to their limit for another in need. This is what *shlichus* is all about.

However, the *shlucha*, a woman emissary, holds a lot more on her shoulders. Not only does she have the responsibility of raising her family, standing by her husband and trying to uplift him as well, but also on *shlichus*, it is the job of a *shlucha* to help raise her community as her spiritual children in all things that they need. There is no regard for the time or hour that she is being called because that is her job as a *shlucha*.

the little house
two blocks away

What's best isn't always comfortable,
and what's comfortable isn't always best.

the sun was peeking in through the window, with the curtains
flowing to the happy tune of the wind. Loud laughter and learning filled
an abode in a community. How peaceful and homey everything looked.
Who would ever think that this was a unique domain, a rented house
representing a place for all to feel welcome?

Sitting around the tables were educated women who dealt out hard
questions, embraced honest answers, and ignited a *rebbetzin* who relished lively discussion.

After a few hours, what seemed like the perfect day for an emissary
came to an abrupt end. Just moments before, I felt like a lighthouse
illuminating warmth and floating in a vision. It then soured into a thick
fog without a glimmer of hope.

My friend and I, who were eagerly sharing and reminiscing about
some of our collected experiences, gently pulled up to a very diminished, small-scale home.

The lantern alive within me turned to an insignificant limp ember
as I was rudely awakened to my own reality. I had to remember what
I purposely tried to forget and rarely thought about: my own physical
discomforts as an emissary.

Emissaries' dreams and visions are unique and are in accordance with
the wants and needs in their lives. The back burner fills with really

justified and painfully needed things and becomes like an overstuffed closet bursting open for relief. When times get desperate, there is sometimes no choice other than to reluctantly accede to a growing family's demands.

Regularly, the routine flavored with worries, wants, and even necessities went into a chest for later. The explosions of negativity that tried to pour in were sealed shut with the gentle reminders of an emissary's role in life.

However, for my friend, her face and reaction said it all. It was one moment of me being her friend, her *rebbetzin*, teacher, and mentor, to then follow her eyes, which looked at a house so small that even a little old lady on her own would find it too cramped to live in.

Our teeny-tiny dwelling came collapsing in all around us from challenging obstacles, for this was no place for an emissary to live. However, we gifted our rented house to our community and had accepted that we would have to exist in only five hundred square feet because we could not afford both dwellings.

I then waved goodbye to my shocked and defeated friend. It was she who understood our cherished work, but she left with a bad taste in her mouth. Our friendship was close, and having recognized her frown, my mood, which was so on fire with positivity, then turned to embarrassment and self-pity.

I shook my head, thinking to myself that this woeful mood wouldn't halt the fireworks of an accomplished day. I hurriedly swept the remnants of regret away with brutal force. I then opened the door to children: my little souls who were smiling at me.

In a utopian world, giving and sharing become our fiddling, similar to an old Jewish grandmother who wants to validate each one by thinking about them and looking them over. Can there really be comfort in *shlichus* (a position or place where emissaries live)? We build up our community, but don't we need to be uplifted as well?

It was after a few too many years of squishing and squeezing into a few hundred square feet that this, in turn, tilted our view slightly, and we began gently pushing ourselves to peek outside of our own uncomfortable lifestyle.

The concept of privacy was not in the cards for us, and our living arrangements had taken many turns through three homes. Our first place began with the uninterrupted stay of our two-year-old in our room. Then in our next tiny abode, our private quarters opened up into our living room, where we acquiesced that it should be our family room by day and then our bedroom at night.

Finally, on our last stop, my husband and I took upon ourselves to sleep in a closet. When we held the door closed tightly enough, it would finally relent and stay shut.

It became the ultimate game to figure out creative fits where each of our four kids could sleep in a two-bedroom home. We became so accustomed to living in such tight quarters that it barely was a difficulty anymore.

Perhaps most people would have put their foot down and arranged for a proper dwelling, but we came last, and those in need came first in our vision that we had for ourselves as emissaries. However, even for us with our idealistic views on life, the time had come to leave our many years of being apartment dwellers behind; the decision had to be made because I became pregnant with our fifth child.

Finally, pure chance or a case of real Divine Providence embraced us. We met this really nice middle-aged realtor, who remembered my husband teaching Torah at the university and had compassion on us. She really made it her top priority to find us the best possible place.

She would schedule meetings for us to sit with her and tell her what a reasonable price would be for us, but I kept pushing them off because I didn't want to put our financial promise given to the Chabad house at risk.

Around the time we met this realtor, it finally happened: someone wanted to buy us a house. We were shocked, but with gratitude accepted the gift. Within a few months, we started looking into finding a real place for ourselves.

The very idea that we would have something this grand of our own felt beyond our mind's grasp. We eagerly ran from house to house to see which one would claim us as its new homeowners, but to no luck; nothing claimed us, and we felt tragically forgotten.

Then, one day it happened: a house was found that sounded so beautiful we hardly dared to come to see it. On the outside, it was a mansion with pillars and a high intricate balcony. I felt like I was a queen coming home to my castle.

The entrance to this castle had a beautiful and exquisite foyer with an old but modern look and feel. As we walked and turned one corner and then another, we then came to the woman's favorite place: the kitchen—a place of secrets, laughs, and whispers.

After a few more spacious steps, we came into the living room. It was the perfect space: a spot for all the kids to sit, play, and enjoy each other's company without crowding.

Yet the best place of all was an office in which French doors and windows created an ambiance so elegant, yet businesslike, that I became eager to say yes that very minute!

I tried hard to calm my excitement, for I was only half of the coin. My husband, instead, was taken aback by all this elegance. He didn't feel comfortable even sitting down in the office. It felt wrong to him, and he was ready to leave. So, I thanked the realtor profusely and told her we would think about it, and we left.

My husband began to get comfortable with what he envisioned would be a long conversation. He took a deep breath and, in a gentle voice, explained that for a rabbi, it was too much. The community needed to be able to approach him at all times, even in his home.

I couldn't believe my ears. We had gone through years of squishing in a two-bedroom apartment and having nowhere to move, forcing us to be super productive in the day and extra quiet at night (since the apartment was so small, even speaking with a normal voice could awaken all the children). I was floored that his view and mine were so different, like night and day.

I felt like I caught lightning in a bottle and never wanted to let go, but I knew that the dream, the stars, and the bottle were beyond my reach and always would be in my obsession with the mansion. I couldn't force my husband to embrace a house that he didn't want. I also knew his words were true and spot on.

There was no choice because I wouldn't force the issue. Before it even began, the conversation was over for me; a rabbi must feel comfortable in his own home.

We started looking for more houses, and each one had its own unique problems. It began to seem futile to keep looking, and we reluctantly resigned to wait for the next year.

Finally, it happened. A house was found two blocks away from the Chabad house, and we decided to look at it. I was quite disappointed. It was not elegant and had no French doors, and space would have to be calculated to perfection to make each room count. It looked ugly on the surface, but it had what we needed to fit our large family and not one hairbreadth more.

So, I played a chess game in my mind. Is it what I need or what I want? The victory came fast, for the place had everything my family needed, so wants would have to come later.

My husband, on the other hand, fell in love with the house two blocks away. He loved each room and even told me how we could repaint and make it all work out well.

I agreed that this would be the place, and sure enough, the house grew on me too. The rooms were painted to my liking, and the furniture claimed the rooms to be ours. The basement became our kids' homeschooling room, and the office became our common domain where we would take turns sharing and caring for its little space.

Yet, the best part of having a cozier place is that my kids were always in my eyes' view. I love to watch the kids walk to shul on Shabbos and see the Chabad house sign from my porch steps, although I definitely miss the mansion's elegance and luxury.

Sometimes, I imagine how great it would have been, but it was too much for our family, and perhaps we would have gotten stuck in that big house and not care about fulfilling the real dreams of *shlichus*.

the haircut that couldn't be undone

A magical day is marked, and a crowd is invited.

it's the community's dream to be a part of each big and little holiday that is celebrated out of the Chabad house: a house for all. They mark it on their calendars and wait excitedly with restlessness for each special day to come.

An *upsherin* (first haircut for a boy of three) is marked with a pen, markers, and most importantly: bated breath. The Chabad family's eager anticipation is most welcome as we all wait in unison for the event to begin.

However, after three long years of tangles, curls, and our close community's warm compliments for our little son, I, like most mothers, had a hard time parting with my little son's hair and what it meant to me.

He is now no longer my little boy, but a boy coming of age for *cheder*, his school: no more little ponytails, hugging my skirt, or feeling assured that all is alright in his little world.

My little son, a big boy, would feel ready for life. I, like most mothers, would wait eagerly to be called if I was needed. To the one observing, it was like magic: when I wasn't called, I would wallow in my own self-pity; when I was called, my mood would change, and I would get busy at my fussing and mothering once again.

This time has arrived, all too soon for me, which will turn the page, and his holy hair will be gone forever. In its place will stand the yarmulke,

14

a symbol of the G-d-fearing Jew, the elevated person, and the proud mensch to be amongst his brethren of today.

The day quickly announced itself, as if the time had run out, and began filling our home with a jittery movement. This continuous rush of liveliness told us that the day was in its element. As Hashem's (G-d) helper, the day began playfully throwing tumultuous waves at me as each hurried hour passed.

My kids were falling over each other and begged for the right outfit to wear for this most special occasion. Their excited hands and feet were dancing to the tune of the "twelve verses" which are a Chabad custom to recite at such times of joy as these.

In the midst of all my rushing and getting each child settled, my husband got a long-needed haircut by his very close and dear friend. His friend, known for his excellent haircutting skills, had my full confidence and agreement. The two continued to talk and hastened their steps to greet us all in the car.

One would think: On the morning before an event? Are you kidding me? However, I knew it wouldn't interfere with my preparations for the program, for by the time my boys finally allowed me to settle them and find each of them their designated places, the haircut would be long over.

As my husband came outside, I noticed that he went a bit faster than usual and had an extra smile on his face. I thought to myself, *This is wonderful, a great haircut for a great occasion.* When my husband bent his head down to go into the car, my mouth dropped in horror. Everything was wrong with his shortened locks.

Not only was the haircut anything but nice, but half of his head had no hair at all! I couldn't even comprehend what I had just seen—let alone that we were ten seconds away from greeting many happy, eager congregants.

Oh, vey (oh, no)! What would they all think? What could I—or my husband—say? It was over! I was readying myself with many explanations and preparing to be a laughingstock.

His friend looked so ashamed and embarrassed, repeating these words over again, "I have no clue what happened: one second it was a great haircut, and the next second, the good moment was replaced with a bad one! It was like the razor had wings all its own." Breathing very fast, he finally took one long breath, gave up on his explanations, and quieted himself down.

I couldn't say a word because I didn't want to hurt his feelings, and really what could one say? It was a mistake—this mistake on this day—and it could not be undone. The haircut was final, and that was that. The car finally stopped, and we all slowly entered the Chabad house.

The door slammed shut behind us, and the kids, my husband the rabbi, and I began our melody of "hello" and "thank you so much for coming." The pats on our backs and hugs were special, but the little whispers had caught my overprotective eye.

They had noticed the horrible haircut! What was there to say or do? I was embarrassed for my husband and wanted to crawl and hide in another room.

The rabbi continued to shake everyone's hand as if all my worries were exaggerated, and it was me making the situation more than it was. He announced in a calm but excited voice the *upsherin* customs including why it's a special day. His loud voice, full of happy emotions and heartfelt goodness, was enough for all of us to forget for a moment what had happened and to move on with this special, new beginning.

My son then had his beautiful, clean, and lovely *upsherin*, and he became everyone's smile, like a lit chandelier in a dimmed room. He stood there with pride, his head held high, allowing each person to partake in his *mitzvah* and take off a part of his curls.

His brothers and friends loudly and sweetly sang songs and chanted the *pesukim*, the twelve customary verses.

My husband's butchered hair became like an old forgotten tale of how I hoped it would be, and I tried hard to enjoy this great *simchah* (joyous occasion) of ours: my little boy becoming like the rest of the clan.

It seemed before I could even grieve for his gorgeous curls—now forever gone—he was bouncing around and singing loudly with the rest of his people.

Goodbyes were said, and leftover hair was placed in a bag for safekeeping. The last of the footsteps faded in the distance, and I finally had a chance to reanalyze the situation. At that moment, rethinking it all, I deeply admired my husband's calm and composure, a state of mind and being that I knew I could not have accessed.

My husband had me shocked, and I asked him quietly about his new look. My husband looked at me, and then straight ahead. In a very focused but quieter voice, he said that his friend meant well, and it was an accident. His friend seemed embarrassed, and it was necessary to keep moving forward, even if it means going to Chabad house programs looking like this.

My husband then looked straight at me again and said, "Besides, it's just hair, and it will grow back." I saw that his demeanor had slightly changed a bit through actually talking about it, but he had no regrets.

What had happened had happened, and there is no looking back, only moving forward. After all, the rabbi again emphasized, "It's just hair, and it will grow back."

Even though that meant for the next month, or more, as he would go to his classes, hospital and house visitations, Shabbos, Friday nights, and *minyan* mornings, it would be excruciating for me, and any other ordinary person.

However, for him, there was no point in dwelling on the past. There was only time to keep placing one foot in front of the other.

It was just a small obstacle, and maybe not really an obstacle at all if one's mind can empower itself to go beyond a silly accident. After all, it's just hair, and it will grow back.

the kohen's blessing

A blessing from a Kohen is a special thing.

our noses breathed in the smell of pollution that mixed rapidly with the bitter cold of winter. The perfectly gray sky acknowledged our happiness and held a bit of sunshine to the gloom. It was just enough to celebrate a newly engaged couple's romantic walk on the bustling streets of Manhattan.

Our feet worked to balance ourselves to walk straight, for our nerves hung out on our shoulders at all times. This awkwardness was well known between a newly engaged Chassidic Chabad couple.

The shy, stolen looks at one another between each crack on the pavement complemented a love that promised to blossom. It was like two little buds peeking out of their parents' grip with their love being so fresh and pure as it scurries on its clear path of new beginnings. We walked and talked for a few long hours until our feet hurt, and the day turned to an early night.

The world of oblivion is a place for the newly engaged. When we were in our daze of stars for each other; we forgot the most basic necessities. Our hearts raced for a moment, and our thoughts kept trying to remember: Where did we park our rented car?

At first, it was a silly joke, and we took our time to look. After an hour of searching, it then became our primary focus. Up and down the busy streets we looked, but the few little blocks seemed to go on forever. Where is it, we thought. What are we going to do?

Then, to add to our already slim chances of recovering our car, a huge rainstorm made a loud booming entrance to the darkened night. It poured and poured like we were in the middle of the Amazon rainforest. The not-so-fun part of living in New York is that it rains, and when it rains, it feels like a wild cat was left alone in the house to play.

After five minutes stuck in the rain shower, my *chassan* (fiancé) said, "Please let me take you home, and I'll come back to look for it."

I don't know why I felt so bad for my fiancé, but I found myself saying, "It's just a little rain. Come, we'll find it, and I even have an idea of where it is." Sure enough, after turning a simple corner, we found it.

We finally sat in our little rented car—our clothes soaked, my makeup ruined. But instead of being upset, we smiled like silly little kids, looking at each other as newly engaged couples do.

My *chassan* then, in an excited voice filled with astonishment, announced to me, "Today, I found myself a life partner." It was such a powerful moment, and these words became a stepping stone to our many hardships and adverse circumstances that we found ourselves in.

As we sat in the car, he told me what made him follow me to where the car was even though we looked around the area many times. He said, "It was the verse of Avraham being told to listen to Sarah's voice. It kept replaying in my head like a broken record player, and I then understood that we would find the car through your help, and we did."

Finally, starving and sopping wet, we came to a kosher restaurant where *Yiddishe* people come to eat. I noticed our entrance caught a few eyes. *Baruch Hashem* (Blessed is G-d), it was quick, and our food arrived, and as we were slowly finishing up, an older man approached our table.

He looked at us with a big smile and said, "I am a kohen, and I have the power within me to bless you." It was surreal to me that the ending to our night was many blessings for our future and our family.

Many people bless each other or receive blessings from very holy rabbis, but *Hashem* (G-d) also gives kohanim the power to bless. The commandment for kohanim to bless others helps us tremendously in good times and bad, and even just day-to-day living.

A blessing from a kohen is an extraordinary thing because he is a conduit from Hashem. The kohen is a messenger to give blessings from G-d, regardless of stature; a kohen's blessing is a great gift of love and kindness that one can receive for free.

I don't know why he blessed us, and I didn't ask, but I thanked him for it. Perhaps it was the fact that we were soaking wet and my makeup was running, or maybe because we were still smiling through it all. Who knows, but it was a very surreal experience and a special one at that.

the first chabad house

Knowing something and experiencing it
are two completely different things.

from a very young age, I lived and breathed the idea of *shlichus*.
Shlichus is the position and place where emissaries go out to live.
However, being the daughter of emissaries is very different from being
an emissary yourself. This life is putting your whole essence, your whole
self, into each moment to make that instance special and pure.

When I first arrived at our old, rented house, it was our only option;
no other houses were for rent in this part of the neighborhood. So, as
I slowly walked my way through the ranch house, I looked intently at
each hidden corner and listened closely to the floorboards creaking
under my New York shoes.

It was then that I imagined a day in a real emissary's life, where
dreams formed, ideas presented, and patterns filled with plans took off.
Unlike other people, when a couple departs on *shlichus*, their entire day
is gifted to their community.

We can be putting kids to bed, reading a book, or even just conversing
with each other when suddenly, a light switch turns on, and everything
else is forgotten. Our surroundings disappear, and all that is in front of
our eyes is this new objective.

It happened quickly—poured out from an hourglass that was frozen
in time to being thrown into a world of acceleration. *Shiurim* (classes)
were like dice tumbling, each one after the other, with every class falling
gently into place.

It was a Thursday night, and my husband announced that there would be a Torah class this evening. Well, the excitement grew, and soon afterward came the knocks at the door.

Meanwhile, the usually very organized *rebbetzin* had totally forgotten the occasion. Since I was bathing the children, the people in my living room had gone unnoticed, and the beautifully packed room had eyes only for us.

It was definitely one of those moments—my boys came out wrapped in their towels in front of all of our guests. Thankfully, my husband continued his discussion, regardless of the entertainment.

After that lapse of judgment, it became crystal clear to me that I needed to start looking for a private and separate home of our own. I wanted there to be professionalism in the Chabad center, that would function as a public domain that everyone knew was theirs. It was an easy conclusion to come to, but it felt like searching for a needle in a haystack to actualize.

My husband, by then, had accustomed himself to the children being in the background. Some might argue that the noise even helped us prepare for our *shiurim*. This new step would be incredibly challenging, especially in the middle of nowhere. It would mean hours and even nights of being apart, because my husband would prepare his *shiurim* in the Chabad center.

Unfortunately, we had no choice; our *shlichus* needed to blossom. So, we began searching for a place of our own. Finally, given our limited budget, a five hundred square-foot apartment became our destination.

We opened the door, took in an eyeful of space, and then quickly scurried out. My husband's eyes said it all, but his words made it real: "I told you that it would be too small for us." Perhaps my determination had a horsepower of its own, and five minutes later, I re-entered the cube.

However, the second time that I walked inside, I pictured the Rebbe with me. So, it clearly became, "When are we moving in?" It was a tough time physically, but emotionally, our excitement knew no bounds. We now had a separate dwelling which allowed us to really focus on our *shlichus*.

Winters here can be frigid. They even have a name for our town: the Frozen Tundra. I knew that to establish a real Jewish community, sacrifices of living comfortably must be made. So, this tiny little box then became our home.

Each Friday night, I walked to the Chabad House in the freezing rain, snow, and ice. The ice was often so thick and slippery that the kids and I had to follow my husband like little ducklings. We would walk in a neat little row and kept falling on the ice until we all came inside.

Perhaps because we had to forfeit all of our luxuries, I loved it even that much more. Time flew by, and in just a few short years, we outgrew the little old Chabad house.

It was the promise of tomorrow that held the day's mood, and it took turns with our verdict. As I packed up the last boxes and looked around at the open space, it felt like the memories we were leaving behind were like a pool full of colors that changed with each splash.

So we started looking for a new place that could fit all of the people we wanted to be part of the Chabad family and also all the tentative souls who still had yet to be touched by an emissary.

the teenage daughter
i never had

Words that come from the heart penetrate the heart.

it was a few years after she left, but my heart couldn't stop thinking of her and where she was going. I wished that I could go back into my memories and replace the wrong word for the right one, to show this young lady that I cared.

I might have been her *rebbetzin*, and she, my congregant, but to her, I was her older friend who came running when she was in need, and to me, she was the teenage daughter that I never had.

As with most mothers and daughters' arguments, there is this battle of which direction she should take or how she should steer herself, and I felt many times like many mothers of teenagers: completely emotionally drained.

I wanted to help her with life, family, marriage, and peace of mind. I remember scribbling down lists for her and her husband—how to divide the chores equally—and hoping with bated breath that some good would come of it.

I was worried about her marriage. Tired of her husband and due to their arguments, she was sleeping on our couch, and there was no solution in sight. I gently tried to get through to her in our weekly get-togethers, but it seemed that she was only half-listening. Instead, she would fantasize about being free of all responsibility.

It was because of this concern that a deep fear grabbed me as I watched her knee-deep in a shaky marriage that sank deeper with each argument about freedom from responsibility.

The mother within me kept popping out each week in our discussions, like an overly-eager jack-in-the-box that I had to force back into the box. I tried to explain to her that compromising and being fully committed is the greatest gift she could contribute to the hardest job of all: being a wife and a mother.

Our conversations seemed to go in circles, leaving us both frustrated with no real outcome. Each quality conversation ended where she seemed to smile and nod, but she kept returning to the same questions: Why should one stay married, and why is being a mother important?

I felt like most days I was tap dancing in front of an audience, but my shoes didn't line up to the beat, and instead, I had acquired two left feet. My mind found no peace, and I worried about my adopted daughter constantly. I probably worried way more than I needed to, but we know this struggle of the Yiddishe mama all too well.

My mind would race laps around itself, trying to come up with practical solutions, but the harder I tried, the farther away the answers felt. I, knowing of her battle with G-d, knowing of her abhorrence to motherhood, and knowing of her feelings of being cheated out of her teenage youth, finally began to understand what she really sought.

She came from her country when she was only twenty years old with two children and all the hardships and physical discomforts of living in the Frozen Tundra. It seemed, before she even settled in, that every argument from her side was made not to have to be a caring mother, wife, daughter, and friend. She threw in the towel way before the time that most others would, and it became apparent to me that even friendship can take its toll on one who is overwhelmed.

It seemed that she really wanted a break from responsibility, even if there was a price to pay. All of her complaints about G-d were emotionally motivated. All she really needed from me was a good friend, a friend who cared unconditionally, who would ask a few questions and require no effort from her side.

I was sitting quietly on my couch after a long Friday afternoon and finally acquiesced to my feet's desire to rest. I was sending out *Shabbat Shalom*'s ("Have a good Shabbos" messages) and began to feel self-pity. Sometimes, my personal good Shabbos messages were glanced over and left unanswered. It felt like I didn't exist, that no one could be bothered to respond.

I quickly checked my phone and saw a new response; it was from her: a young woman who had moved back to Israel and felt conflicted about a woman's role in Judaism. It was her battle within to see if there really was a G-d.

I held my breath, unsure of how I could help her, as I looked down at her note. Yet, instead of needing my help, she was messaging me with beautiful words, kind words, and caring words that were words of the soul.

She had written to me in her note that I had changed her life, and she was not ready yet to be more observant but was open to maybe, someday, starting slowly, sooner rather than later.

However, her most personal words touched me; she was a reluctant daughter who was writing to her adopted mother. She said that she was grateful for my kindness and our long back-and-forth discussions. She then wrote words that would be difficult for anyone to write, but for her impossible. But there they were: she always loved me as her friend from the very beginning.

It might sound silly to the outsider and perhaps lost in translation to the newcomer, but our friendship, and the many sacrifices that I've made to help her and her family, turned those words into golden words. They were words that grew wings and danced like butterflies to the trained eye.

She continued to write that my kindness towards others forced her to get in touch with her own attribute of kindness, which was hard for her to do because she didn't have a lot growing up. Regardless, she decided that helping more people was something she wanted to explore. Her message was truly uplifting for me, and I felt that I finally made an impression and fulfilled the dream that *shluchim* are meant to fulfill.

I remember sitting with her in my dining room. She was at one side of the table, and I was at the other. I foolishly believed I could make a difference by logically convincing her that Torah is true and G-d exists.

As much as she argued from a logical standpoint—like all atheists do—she was emotionally motivated. Then it dawned on me that this was the reality behind all her questions and confrontations with me; it was all because of her grief and ups and downs in life. The decision to stand with G-d and her religion was a huge step, especially for her, having grown up observant without having many of her questions answered.

I asked her once why, if she didn't believe in G-d, she would celebrate the holidays. She replied, "Well, life and our culture are part of the holidays, and I want my daughters to have them in their lives."

I continued, "So you want your little girls to be observant and keep Shabbat, correct?"

"No," she replied. "Not at all. That is not what I'm saying. Only if my daughters decide to."

"I see," I said. "So, college and school are mandatory, but their life as a Jew is only if they decide?"

"Correct," she said to me. "Their religion is only mandatory if they want it, but school is necessary because they need to get a degree."

Standing before me was a daughter of Sarah, Rivkah, Rochel, and Leah; besides, she grew up *frum* (observant in the faith). How could I convince her not to give up on G-d or her people?

I realized, for now, after two years of learning with her, that very little progress had been made, or so I thought. Perhaps, I should alter my approach. I clearly needed just to be her friend instead of her adopted mother.

It happens to many; often times, one wants to help people, and a different hat needs to be placed on one's head: a mother, a sister, a friend, or a confidant. It's hard to know which hat to wear at the right moment.

So, whenever I was needed, I came running, and time continued to slide by, and her beautiful little Jewish daughters went to the local *goyish* (non-Jewish) school. The happy part of this terrible decision was that she agreed to send her daughters to Hebrew School each week to learn a bit about their heritage and Judaism.

One day, her younger daughter came crying to me and asked me to draw her the cross. I said, "Leah, you're Jewish, and a Star of David is what Jewish people draw when they're sad. Can I draw you a Star of David?"

"No, No. Please, *morah* (teacher), draw me the cross. My teachers always draw it for me when I'm sad."

I had to turn away and force myself not to cry. I then started to draw a few hearts, and then she wanted more hearts and even asked for the Star of David. I then began *davening* (praying) with the group, and she sang along and clapped her hands to songs she knew so well.

I might have won that day, but I knew this battle was one of many, and perhaps, I might lose the ultimate war with my adopted daughter. I didn't want to think about her girls marrying out of our faith. So, I tried to keep my mind busy with other things.

After some time, we stumbled into our conversation again. Does Hashem (G-d) exist? As she joined our cooking class to help us cook for Shabbos, education came up, and she adamantly refused to send her daughters to a Jewish school and told me outright that they could have non-Jewish boyfriends if they wanted, as long as they were happy. I tried to explain the outcome of intermarriage and how both sides become hurt and confused, but to no avail.

She was like a burning fire refusing to be pacified. I closed my mouth and made sure I was focused only on my cooking. Sometimes, silence is the strongest of words. Pictures and pictures filled an album of solutions, but my mind was turned off, and I continued to help the other ladies.

A few more years had passed since our attempt to reignite the discussion, which was for me an attempt to argue the case for her and her kids to stay *frum*, but the chance never came. It was a hectic time for us, and she announced to me that she would be going to Israel for a few months and that we should get together.

I was so excited to host her and her family and decided on a good old barbecue. We said our hellos, and she started helping me with the salads and fruit. She began with her usual questions and derogatory remarks about Torah and being *frum*.

I changed the topic and asked her about her plans. We were interrupted by the call that the food was ready. We sat down together with our kids entertaining us—from wild screams to cute Jewish songs and a thousand questions about the *parsha* (weekly Torah portion). It was finally time to go, and we ended off with a bang of fireworks.

I said my goodbyes and went to start cleaning up. Suddenly, she rushed into my house and hugged me tight—she who *never* hugs or shows much affection to anyone. It blew me away; she began choking up, crying, and telling me that she would miss me so much. I said that I would miss her, but we would see her in a few months.

She then said, "You don't understand. I'm not coming back to America ever again. I'm leaving for good. My older daughter needs a special school, and my younger daughter can't stay here by herself even with my husband, who will join us later. Instead, I will take them both, and they will come to learn Torah with me in Israel." I looked at her as if she had just fallen off the moon or if I was in an alternate universe.

She said that she would keep in touch, and she was happy that I pushed her to get herself a degree to work in Israel. Now, this time I had tears in my eyes. She was changing so slowly that she didn't even realize it. I vowed to stay in touch and slowly walked her back to her car. As they drove away, I wondered for the first time what changes really lay ahead for them.

The words on the screen spoke volumes about her mindset and where she was really headed. She was growing up, and her kids are slowly becoming more observant in their faith. She was lagging only a few feet behind them and was catching up quickly. A few more turns and I would allow myself to remove my mother hat more often and replace it with just a caring friend.

an adopted grandfather

Sometimes a person needs to ask for help even if
he prefers to be the one giving, for it enables others
to climb the ladder of life.

it was our first winter here on our *shlichus*, and before we could understand that this was not New York, blizzard after blizzard mounted itself
in front of our house. It was almost like the snow was trying to intro-
duce itself to us and make sure we realized it was there.

The wheels in our heads started turning, trying to come up with
solutions but nothing stuck. It was like pulling a rope in many different
directions, but the rope would not budge.

How would we accomplish anything in such weather? Five seconds in
the snow and we were freezing, covered head to toe in fluff.

As *shluchim*, comfort always came along like a little sister begging to
be heard, but our dedication to our mission tuned it out. Somehow, we
needed to figure out a way to be many steps ahead even if the weather
kept us many steps behind.

Unfortunately, even with our strengthened positivity, we began to
realize that we needed outside help: an extra pair of hands. Finding
where and who to turn to in a new place became an overwhelming burden that we tried not to think about.

We were so excited to be leaders in our community that simple necessities were absent from our life. At the time, we still were living in our
rented house that quickly became a makeshift Chabad house.

Our ranch had only two bedrooms, one for us and one for our kids. We started having religious services in our living room, followed by a family sit down for a warm cozy Shabbos meal.

Shabbos was almost upon us when we received a phone call from a kashrut supervisor, a *mashgiach*. He sounded worried and was looking for a Chabad house where he could stay for Shabbos. So we welcomed him into our home without quite realizing that we didn't have much space where he would be able to retire for the night.

After quietly schlepping, moving, sweating, and rearranging all of our children's places, we squeezed him into our only other tiny room with an air mattress on the floor. The absence of space and luxury left our guest with the company of our children's toy box and the Rebbe's pictures on the wall.

We felt really embarrassed. There was only a little bit of room and not even a proper bed for this Jewish man. We would've preferred to hide in our children's toy chest than to face him in this sticky circumstance.

However, we pushed forward towards positivity, for that was all we had in our home at the time. It was useless to rehash what we could have had if we didn't have it. He didn't seem to care or mind the sleeping quarters. Rather, it seemed that he was content and relaxed in our home.

The children then took over our room, and Shabbos charm and ambiance made its jubilant entrance into our Chabad house. It was an inspiring twenty-five hours where my husband and I felt more like our guest was an old friend rather than a nice kind man that we'd just met. Before long, a comfortable, genuine Shabbos with the *mashgiach* became our weekly reunion.

He would come to visit us like an old grandfather, wondering how the kids were and how we were doing. It was something new for us because most people have their own troubles hanging over their shoulders. There was rarely time for someone to befriend us, let alone be able to look at us as people, as friends, and as individuals.

Instead, we became the spiritual leaders, parents, and comforting presence to a growing community in need. Through their hardships and urgent need to feel at peace, this kindness and fellowship became forgotten. They, instead, wanted us to take the reins and set right what they needed. They were our spiritual children, and we became obliged and eager to fulfill our community's every need.

Yet, this old grandfather was unique, different, and special. The door would come swinging open to another one of his hellos. He would never come empty-handed and always had a basket filled with trinkets, cheese, or some special kosher food.

He would pop in and ask me how I was doing and how I was feeling. These few words brightened up my week. His kind, fatherly presence made us feel like we mattered to him.

This concept was so strange to me, for I had already entrenched the idea in my head that this type of kindness was our right and ours alone. It was our job and responsibility to be there at all hours for each person in need. To be met by a stranger who cared so much was unusual and definitely a breath of fresh air.

One day, the thought popped into my mind of asking this *mashgiach* to help bring food to our community. My husband was concerned that it might be a bit of a chutzpah, but I was determined that the community was waiting for us to institute some real changes. So, we waited for him to pack his stuff and walked him out to his car.

Favors, favors, and no show of hands—favors are usually reserved for a small group of close-knit friends who care enough to busy themselves to help one another. It was a risk, but I was desperate. So, I courageously boldened myself to ask him for a favor. My husband stood beside me, and it became easier to ask.

I smiled shyly but boldly said, "Since you are coming from a place of many Jewish markets, can you please pick up our order?" I held my breath; my mind was racing to find a solution for Chanukah, and we were eager not to let anyone down. He agreed to pick up our order, and he brought it to us to our total surprise and delight.

Our very first order went through about three different hands until we met it on our friend's driveway. We couldn't believe our eyes, and our gratitude knew no bounds for this kashrus supervisor.

The snow was piled higher than ever, even too much for this "Frozen Tundra," and his car's tires began to slide and roll. The car was desperate to find its place amongst its peers.

Finally, there were helping hands that came out of nowhere to unload the car before it was turned off. Bags started spilling from all sides with chicken, meat, *knishes* (potato-filled bourekas), yogurts, doughnuts, *latkes* (potato pancakes), and everything needed to survive without a kosher store.

Then, it happened that another time of empty pantry, fridges, and freezers came too soon. We needed our order of kosher food once again. I buzzed many phones of different helpers, but the snow prevented them from helping us, and we felt inclined to ask our adopted grandfather once again.

So it was, and without hesitation, he answered in a booming voice, "Yes, of course, I want to help!" He agreed, and pretty soon, we would wait for his little blue car to come each week for us to have food. The next challenge was then to fit the food into our freezers. Our minds were at peace, and life became a little less difficult.

Time passed, and our helper and adopted grandfather became very close with us. We invited him into our behind-the-scenes life and into the different small apartments that we had over the years. He even started bringing different kinds of trinkets for the boys, and they, and we, were happy.

I waited each week to hear him tell us a story, phrase, or interesting tale that he had learned from his job. His happy attitude made our weeks fly by, and the examination of his newfound tool of positivity made a deep impression on us. It stood beside us in helping our family and keeping our community happy.

After asking him many times where he discovered this wonderful approach to life, he shared something personal and private with us. It was a moment where one couldn't take back what was said. He was a cancer survivor, and his routine became very difficult for him. Each day he tried to take the positive from life and had little regrets.

It happened that, with time, we built a relationship with his kids as he did with ours. The *mazel tovs* (congratulations) on special occasions were said with joy. We spoke to each one of his kids or ours, to that one and this one, that would go overseas to a dangerous country. We held our breath like he did when they went, and the loneliness of *shlichus* seemed paused for a time.

It suddenly happened that he wasn't able to visit as often, and he was more withdrawn than usual. I asked him if everything was alright, and he set up a meeting with my husband and me. It was strange to hear of this meeting that came out of nowhere. So, we sat down at the table, and I offered him some tea and cookies.

He looked at us, gently playing with his long white beard. After a while, he took us off pause and said that he was sick again. This time he wasn't sure if he would be all right. We were devastated and broken to hear such horrible news. "What can we do?" we hurriedly said, feeling completely and utterly helpless. He said that he would see how things would go for now, and we should focus on our work.

Time took its turns and worry filled us all, both families—his and ours—until finally, surprises filled with open miracles occurred before our eyes. Hashem (G-d) once again showed us that He controls the world, and this adopted grandfather was saved. He still comes to visit us from time to time, and when he goes home, we eagerly await his next visit.

At this point, we have a kosher store nearby and a house of our own with a nice room where he can sleep for Shabbos and where there is a *minyan* weekly, accompanied by a warm Shabbos meal. This time, we can give him little trinkets and ask him how he is feeling. We know that no matter how long the absence, the connection between our adopted grandfather and his kids is forever.

going deaf in the prime of life

G-d is carrying you even in the hardest of times.

the banging, the chanting, the blotting out of Amalek's name triumphed. Among the laughter, the songs, the tables full of smiles and warmth, a beautiful couple sat quietly and at peace. It was their world of bliss, and unbeknownst to them, it would be their last for a while. Soon they would face the biggest challenge of their wedded life.

A sound went out: a loud, constant, painful ringing in his ears—the heroes of his day. It was like a bee constantly buzzing, which made it hard to hear the kids and family.

"My beautiful wife, what will she say? How can I tell her that I've become a deaf man in the prime of my life?" His head began to throb with a headache of nerves that made him unable to organize his thoughts.

"What letters from those words to use? What thoughts can I think? It is useless and pointless to try to hold onto hope." He felt that his ship had already sailed, and the little beacon of hope left in his heart and mind was flickering out into the unknown.

Round and round, his mind played this game of unwanted self-pity. It felt wrong to this selfless young man because these new, unwanted thoughts were like a foreigner on his porch steps. However, the questions were nagging at him and gave him no reprieve.

"When will hope return?" He did not know and felt too numb to care about positivity and allowing a torch to shine on the world around him.

It felt unfair that life had handed him such a rotten deck of cards. He had nowhere to go but to accept this new reality.

His ears were the magic in his day! They were so important to each big or little situation that he was needed for. He never really thought about how much he depended on his ears to know what was really going on, and how they would be thrown to waste, like an unused wood-burning stove in the summer.

"My friends—what will they say?" He thought to himself. "It's my job to listen to them, to laugh, cry, share, and comfort them. How will I even be able to, when my ears no longer hear their whispers or cries?"

He felt ashamed to face his whole world, the world that made him himself, which included everyone and everything except his rabbi. He felt close to his rabbi and appreciated his advice. He liked that the rabbi would give him absolute care and friendship no matter what happened, with no strings attached.

It was a whole life of giving and sharing gone from something we take for granted each day, as we burden ourselves to grieve over other things.

One day, as this man came home, he quietly sat on his couch, and he announced to his wife that he could barely hear anything at all. He was very distraught and felt sorry for himself, but still, in trepidation, he held his breath to hear his soulmate's reaction.

The terrible news hit her like a tornado on steroids. She felt worried and upset inside, knowing that things would forever be changed, but from his perspective, she sat there calmly, holding his hand and whispering words of endearment and comfort.

She knew what was at stake, but felt that Hashem (G-d) had a bigger plan for them, and this was merely a test. She felt the inner struggle to suppress her deep sense of worry, and she refused to allow herself the chance to grieve or feel bad for herself.

This wasn't about her, and it wouldn't help anyone if she sunk low and gave into the temptation of giving up, even with this being the norm for what her new reality would be.

She then echoed courageous thoughts to him and said, "Let's wait and see what the doctor says."

He replied, feeling defeated and broken with self-pity seeping into his tone, "How can you be so calm? Everything is not going to be OK! I could lose my job! What if hearing aids won't work? Who would want a cripple like me around them as their friend?"

He continued, more exasperated than ever: "I'm also very concerned about how you are going to feel about staying married to me! What if I'm just a burden on you?" He stopped for a minute, holding his head and taking a deep breath.

He then lowered the volume and tone a bit and continued, "An older person can say that he's older, but this is the prime of my life, and maybe you won't want to stick around."

"How can you say that?" his faithful wife replied. "We are in this together, and I'm not going anywhere. We will figure out what needs to happen. Please, let's focus on other things for now."

Even though she felt hopeless herself, she knew she had to be the pillar, the strong one, to hold her husband up in his time of devastation and mental anguish.

A few months passed, and the appointment came and went, but the results were not good. He had moderate hearing loss and needed hearing aids. The new hearing aids seemed to help disguise the condition, but it was a difficult situation.

Slowly, after some more time passed, his job and life in general became much easier for this man. He met with his rabbi regularly, and it helped his state of mind. However, the worry of what would still be weighed on his shoulders constantly, and he felt no peace.

Sometimes in life, things are thrown at a person, and it seems beyond his or her ability to deal with it. Just remember that you are not alone; G-d is always carrying each person even in the hardest of times.

How lucky this man was to have such a pillar of a wife who didn't care about the stigma or the changes that would occur and what would be with his life. She knew that her husband needed her and needed her to be strong, regardless of the worry she felt inside.

They are happily married and truly appreciate one another—even more so than ever before. The relationship has matured from love to a profound love and caring for one another.

Perhaps, that is what G-d desired all along: for this close couple to become even closer through a difficult test that was thrown their way. Through all of his darkness and brief moments of feeling alone, this man knew, with his wife by his side, that he was never truly alone.

The story continued, and miraculously his hearing started to return slightly, and the ringing in his ears did end up going away. However, his wife decided to help her other half by playing a silly game.

She claimed that her hearing wasn't so good and even pretended she couldn't hear when they were in front of company. It was all pre-planned so that people would speak up and allow her husband to save face.

This man started to feel at peace again and enjoyed regular, day-to-day activities. It soon became the norm not to feel his nerves wrapped tightly on his shoulders, like a prickly, tight sweater. Instead, he felt a deep calm quicken its pace to catch up to him.

As time passed and his hearing improved even more, he picked up steam in all things that he once rejected, and life became treasured even more so than ever before.

It then appears that even a deaf man at the prime of his life can overcome many obstacles thrown at him. His wife, his lighthouse, turned her back on the grief that begged to come inside their little home. Through her unbreakable courage, she shooed away the thoughts of "what will be" and replaced them with lanterns of calm and hope.

a table full of emotions

Life is about giving yourself over as a leader
to your community in big and little ways.

the tables are filled, laughter can be heard, and a promise to an old leader (the Lubavitcher Rebbe) kept, so why does the mood change to blue as I sit so content with dreams fulfilled? What am I missing that my heart wants to claim?

I think for a moment and wonder, can it be something this silly? It is a desire for attention, like I'm being ignored, even when I cause the tables to be filled with good feelings, happiness, and joy.

I include people who feel forgotten during the week, and I push harder to spend time with our community family. Their fondness for Chabad brings a resolution, and therefore their reaction is to come to feel warmhearted and blessed at a table full of giving and a house that feels like home.

The table is set, and the wine is poured. A joke, a song, a special look between the two of us is made. A look is stolen during the recital of the holy poem to a couple loaned to a community; given over to each other is a look of love and embrace.

Aishes Chayil: a poem, from a book by King Solomon, is cradled in our home, heart, and souls. However, like most special poems, this song has a deeper meaning for us. It means that in the midst of the weekly chaos, we pause from our hectic week for our family's blessed Shabbos to then hold each other with a stolen look across the aisle.

We look at one another for a split second when the wine is being filled in the *bechers,* the special customary cups. Most are busy singing and reading, finally hearing the humming of familiar verses of so long ago. Carefully, hidden in plain sight, do we dare catch each other's eye, for all affection in our world is done behind closed doors.

This most precious of hidden looks is to keep us focused on our Shabbos table and pay the guests the attention that they so deserve, while at the same time sharing a reserved and affectionate moment with a song that unifies the home and captures the hearts of hopeless romantics.

Sometimes, I can feel the question come sneak up on me: What about our desires, emotions, and the feelings in our hearts? Must they always be put aside? It seems so hard—especially when the table is beautifully set and the ambiance is a romantic moment in the making.

Yet, as spiritual workers, we never take a break, and the very thought of wanting a moment to ourselves can feel almost selfish! I remembered when my oldest, in a silly moment of feeling things were unfair, went to one of the corners of the Chabad house to cry. Both my husband and I, not noticing each other's presence, went to comfort our son.

So there we were, having a family moment in the presence of the *shul* (synagogue). Everyone stopped their little chats and slowly stepped closer with ears angled to listen in and hear our conversation. They were smiling and laughing and even patting our eldest on the back. Our little quiet private family circle became an even bigger public community circle.

I was confused at first that not one of them understood we wanted a moment of privacy. However, to forgive and forget is easy, for I understood they are like our children too, and wanted to be included.

Even if tokens of family get-togethers are special, these moments are meant to remain few and far between, for we as spiritual parents remain focused on our community family.

Many people of all backgrounds and levels of observance come to speak to both of us, sometimes together and at other times individually. It is hard to know, and at the same time good to know, that no matter how special it may seem to have children and family, that Friday nights, holidays, and special occasions are shared with your physical and spiritual children.

On the one hand, how can you complain about children needing you and your love? On the other hand, sometimes you desperately just want to relax and enjoy each step of that moment with each other, to *daven* (pray), and learn just a bit longer than usual, and spend the pure time celebrating in the holiday's special embrace.

I always felt that these feelings were more from my side, the *rebbetzin's* side. As a woman and a more emotional creature, surely these feelings were more from me. However, I was in for a surprise when my husband told me that this is how he felt as well.

It happened to me one time that a friend I hadn't seen for a while came to us for Shabbos. It was a smaller Shabbos with only a *minyan* (ten people) of guests, and I noticed that my boys wanted to be included in my conversation every moment.

My friend's and my every whisper, recalling and reminiscing each little thing that happened in our ten years of knowing one another, mesmerized my kids, who were listening and contributing very enthusiastically, even climbing, hanging, and sitting on our chairs as we adults still sat talking inside them.

They rebelled and went to ridiculous extremes just to get a reaction, a laugh, or a wink. Finally, they settled down. I finished my conversation, cleaned up from the meal, and we said our goodbyes.

My husband seemed a bit quieter than usual, and I asked him what was bothering him. He sat down and confided in me that he felt happy that my friend came and that it was important to help her, for that is *shlichus* (a position or place where emissaries live)." He paused and slowly continued, "That is why we are here, but I missed your company!"

It might sound odd because I was in the room with him, but paying attention to each other for real is the company of the heart. I smiled at him and said, "Finally, after all these years, you told me what I always struggled to understand in my own heart."

Love for each other is felt in many ways, and sometimes it is hard always to share each step in life with our children and spiritual children—even if we wouldn't have it any other way, and that's why we are here. One can argue it makes us better for it, and truly because of it, we treasure and value each other that much more.

We might still be jealous of that special moment that we missed alone, but we cherish and marvel at each moment that we do have that much more. After almost fifteen years of marriage, this couple who was loaned to a community still share and desire a *Chassidishe* (Chassidic) embrace and love.

The sweat, tears, joy, and pain are well worth building a family of children and polishing the jewels (our congregants) in our close community. It seems almost strange with our children and community obligations always keeping us apart from one another that they are what bring us closer together. It is in our search and desire to give to others that we find one another.

my son smashed the shul window

A terrible mistake brought them to cross a line that now they embrace and desire to protect and cherish each day.

a beautiful Saturday night is usually an excuse to take a drive together. We love the feeling of the breeze on our faces, and it was the perfect night for a date, but tonight it would not be. We heard the slamming of doors in our ears, and the following silence was worse than loud screeching tires. Our thoughts were consumed with the day's tragedy, and there was no more room in our minds to change the night's tune.

As I climbed up the stairs and looked closely through the darkness, my eyes took in the damage. There it was: the window—a sad excuse for its former self. The mark was obvious in the silhouette of the remaining few pieces that still stood strong.

Pieces, pieces, so many memories of hard-earned sweat, tears, determination, and this is how it ends up? Light bounced off the crystal pieces with their sharp edges. The floor, glistening with just little streaks of what had represented safety, now became a mess and a headache to absorb. I had to see it for myself, and I carefully walked around the smashed glass.

That morning as I opened the Chabad house door and sat down to work, I looked at the window that once represented light, happiness, and safety. The etched fist imprint brought a fear of what could have happened and thankfulness that in our tiny temple of today, it wasn't an anti-Semitic attack, but just my children throwing one too many punches.

Shabbos felt longer than usual, and my seven-year-old son was having one of his days of not wanting to participate in anything he was offered. He was crying and moping around in his room, and no matter how I pushed him to end his tantrum and rejoin the group, he refused. It was hard with the world on a big time out, and each step I took, trying to spread light and positivity, was challenged and countered even more forcefully than before.

On a regular Shabbos here in our hometown, all the big boys were out the door before nine, and that included my seven-year-old son. Sometimes, he enjoyed the Shabbos *minyan*'s melodies and atmosphere, and other times he would rather curl up under his covers and shut us all out. It didn't help that he was shorter than his five-year-old brother or that he overanalyzed his day-to-day activities with a fine-tooth comb.

Everything was closed during this coronavirus time, and I couldn't let him just hibernate in his room. It was Shabbos, and the boys could at least pray together as a family in the Chabad house, even if that meant pleading, begging, and promising treats just to get him to go out and be a part of the group made up of his brothers.

The more I pushed, the more resistance I received. My older sons gave him a look of "Oh, come on, not again. Can you grow up this time and be a mensch?" However, all the looks in the world didn't help but, instead, aggravated the situation until it felt that the seams would burst open and pour themselves out.

What none of us were counting on was my nine-year-old son. He loved to dress up fancy and wore his shirt tucked into his pants with his Tatty (father) belt and a suit jacket that made him appear older and more sophisticated than his years. He was having none of this tantrum and decided he would fix the situation.

The feeling of excitement and hopefulness was quickly deflated like a popped oversized balloon. His usual grandfatherly nature was absent, and in its place stood a boy his age. My head felt like a pincushion full of needles, as I understood what the result was going to be.

I was trying to figure out a way to stop it, but my son was determined as he will ever be, and there was no stopping his overeager approach. Just what I needed was another fight between them. So, I tried separating them, focusing my older son on *davening* (praying) and finishing his morning routine. It helped for a bit, but by the time the afternoon Shabbos meal ended, he was ready for the second round.

This idea popped into my head; perhaps he can take his little brother to pray at the Chabad house even without services. I still had the boys walk over to pray or learn to keep up their routines and add positivity to their day. So, they both agreed to go and even held hands.

It's what every mother dreams of: kids getting along. One tends to ignore one's own intuition that whispers incessantly like an unwanted neighbor pushing herself through your front door. I sent my oldest son to watch over them, but still, things have a way of getting out of hand, and before I could figure out what went wrong, the rug was pulled out from under me.

My oldest son came home to tell me what happened. I knew it couldn't be good because usually, he likes to pray and study most of the day, so coming home to talk on Shabbos wasn't a good sign.

He kept shaking his head and took the courage to say words that made me feel like I was being punched in the gut: "Mommy, the little boys fought, and his fist punched the window, and the glass shattered into many pieces. It happened so fast while I was praying the afternoon service."

The front door slammed open again before I could even think of an answer of how to respond. The two little boys who were meant to get along and meant to be friends were crying and breathlessly trying to blame one another for what went wrong.

How can I fix this? What did they expect me to do? What magic wand could I use to fix what was broken and to make them understand that there would be consequences for their actions? The question was, how could I get them to realize this so that they would never cross this line again?

Every single day, and on Shabbos too, when the world isn't on pause, I go to the Chabad house with a sense of worry on my shoulders that I must shake off. Will everything and everyone be alright?

It is a deep fear, a real worry that perhaps a terror attack will happen. At night when the streets are quiet, I pray that the mini temple stands protected. I never thought that I had to include my own children into this equation.

After a few hours, I saw my two little sons in different rooms, each having the same reaction. Both of them were sulking and sitting at the edge of their beds, feelings of remorse spewing from their mouths. The house's tone felt quiet and tense, and no one, not even the baby, made noise. I couldn't help myself as a Jewish mother to see how they were doing and how this impacted them.

The tears on their faces said it all; they felt miserable that they broke part of the Chabad House, a little piece of G-d's temple. My oldest son peeked into their rooms and said, "Mommy, we should call a fast day for our family. All the children should wait to eat until noon."

This suggestion surprisingly brought a halt to the crying and a hint of forgiveness for themselves. As their mother, I truly believed that I would never have to worry again after seeing their reactions to what had happened.

Everything happens for a reason, and perhaps this lesson learned will stay close to them. Then they will be more careful with holy places and feel even more connected and appreciative of how they treat one another.

the boy was not mine

Choose, choose life, and choose what's right!

it was early on in our *shlichus*, and we had a small, cozy, crowded Shabbos that week. I chanced to meet a young new father. He was like a wise old owl, telling tales to the little birds in the trees. Every ear and eye was open in eager anticipation of the next words to be spoken. So, naturally, I loved it that my boys found someone who could entertain them.

My husband and I looked at each other in total surprise because this man loved playing with all of our boys. It was like finding a rare stone that you hoped wouldn't get lost.

This new gem of ours was a very talkative, caring, and gentle person. That whole Shabbos, each boy got a turn to ride on his shoulders and was able to hear his silly jokes. He never got bored or annoyed with our children: he was just happy to be there.

After seeing my children's attachment to him, the rainbow of colors in my week became obvious along with the pitter-patter of feet thumping on the hardwood floor; their shrieks of laughter exploded and could even fill up a crowded room. I thought to myself; the children have arrived to play with their favorite trusted owl.

One day, he sat down to talk to my husband and me. He said that his wife really had some serious behavioral issues, involving severe child abuse towards his infant son. Our jaws dropped in shock as he then sadly explained that his wife was the complete opposite of himself.

He desperately needed a job to provide his family with money, so he chose to work in America and had no choice but to leave his wife and family behind. No one wants to be in this type of situation, and keeping in touch can be tiresome, especially when his job begins before the rooster is out. The mentality between here in America and there in South America is very different.

Unfortunately, after his son was born, his wife decided that she did not want her son anymore. Her only way to deal with what she felt was a situation that couldn't be controlled was to thrash out at whatever and whomever she felt was the problem. Eventually, the owl's wife started to blame him for it all. This caused her to start to beat the owl himself and her infant son even more.

As we listened to his tale of woe, we felt forlorn in a chaotic battlefield. It was like being in the midst of war: trenches are dug, but there are no instructions. Where do we go? What do we say? It was a painful experience; the casualties kept on coming, and the war's end was nowhere in sight!

This manual of broken instructions created circles of confusion with a way of thinking that was far from ours. I tried to wrap my head around this story to understand the mother better. I tried to rationalize with her emotional pain, but the clarity I felt turned to a dark, sticky fog.

There was no excuse! It dawned on me that even if she needed help, what she needed didn't explain her behavior and her *camma* (when) didn't explain the *eicha* (how). How could she do such a thing, a daughter of Sarah, Rivkah, Rochel, and Leah?

My head started unraveling like a ball of yarn that hit the floor. I thought to myself, what if every story does not end the same?

I tried to roll the yarn back up, but it was useless, and it got stuck somewhere in the middle. I felt like my hands were tied, and I stood helpless about what I should do, even though social services were involved. Things were still quite difficult, so I decided to do more for the community and my family. I naively hoped that this terrible situation would sort itself out in time.

After two years passed, life moved on: it was so busy that I had even forgotten this man's troubles. One day my husband came suddenly to me, and it seemed urgent. I said, "What happened? What's wrong?" My husband told me that this family's mother had seriously abused her three-year-old boy, and the father, our once trusted owl, became one who lost his voice!

He and his wife were miles apart, distanced inside and out, living in different countries; there was no way he could keep his infant son safe. He decided to go back to South America and bring his little son back with him to the States. However, this meant that his little son, the one he wanted but unfortunately, she did not, had to go with him to America until things calmed down.

His little boy, so frail and tiny, sat quietly in a large, brightly lit room, all alone in a different country and with no one who could even speak his language. The quiet, soft voice only asked for the bathroom and a small bowl of food to eat.

There were no sounds of his laughter or pitter-patter on the hardwood floors. There was no rainbow of colors in his eyes; instead, there were black wells of darkness.

A gloomy sense of where a boy once stood was now replaced with a shadow of his former self. The marks on his head and face were enough to tell us his tale of his mother's shameful, cowardly actions.

Our kind owl, now in real need of our help, would be working full time: there would be no one to be with this little boy. The realization snuck up upon us, and our wheels started slowly turning. As *shluchim*, helping others was like our life and breath. We had to try to find a way.

Could we take the little boy into our home, even for a little while, so that everything going on at the time could calm down? I knew the very idea couldn't be spoken out loud. How could we fit another one into our tiny little apartment?

Could I claim him as my own, and could I love this little boy like my other little boys? Would there be strings attached to the adoption, from his parents, or maybe conditions that I didn't think of? If they wanted only foster care, how could I take him in and then let him go?

Just allowing these thoughts of the back and forth felt like an ice-cold bucket of water hitting me in the face. I started feeling very emotional and worried that I wouldn't be able to figure out a solution for this sweet, abused little boy and that I would have to helplessly hand him over to the wrong hands.

I knew that I could never do this, but I had no choice: I had to take him in and save him from this horrible situation—even if it meant that in the end, my heart would break, and I would only have him temporarily.

I would have to make sure that the time he would be with us would be a qualitative time, a time where a family would love him, and a time where he would laugh each day. I truly was ready to adopt this sweet boy but knew this was not an option because the parents were against it, and I wasn't sure if that was a good sign or a bad sign.

After much thought, I finally agreed to take the boy and have him live with us for a few years, even if it meant that he could go back at any time and to a bad situation. As terrible as his story sounds, everything is up to Hashem (G-d) at the end of the day. Sometimes we must sit back and let Hashem choose one's fate, even if it helps for a little while, or so I convinced myself.

Baruch Hashem (Blessed is G-d), we bumped into the great mazal storm Himself: Divine Providence. After many sleepless, agonizing nights, trying to figure out how to save this little boy from a bad situation, an observant couple volunteered to take him into their large home for a year until things mellowed out.

After many months of serious counseling, the owl's wife was able—with much help—to take her little boy into her home with open arms. It was a process, but she stood firm to break through the problems that had caused her little boy so much emotional and physical pain. She was ready to start again and hoped her little boy could forgive her.

After all of this, it seems trivial to ask, "Are they still married?" So, my husband, in his weekly counseling, asked the question: "Do you still want to be married?" They both hurriedly replied that they wanted to remain married. Even though every week they weren't sure for years. However, once the question of marriage was thrown at them and it sat and ate in their laps, they decided that they really did want to make it work.

It's a lesson to be learned: our work is never finished. This particular family was drowning on all sides; like fixing a leaky roof, when one board is fixed, it doesn't mean that the others are suddenly made of sturdy new wood.

However, slowly but surely, people can be given the reins of endearing kindness. They can then learn how to love, bond, respect, and cherish their loved ones. Over time, one door may open, and another one can finally close.

a diamond
in my living room

The almost forgotten tale started with two half-broken
instruments and ended with a complete symphony.

it's the untold story which begins and ends—a story one could try
to forget and hurriedly look towards tomorrow. The new puzzle seems
perfect both in fit and in measure; the old one was different in lengths
sewn crookedly together.

It's been ten years of giving, helping, and building our community.
There have been ups and downs, but every place has its charm and
warmth that draws one inside.

I remember my husband's words so clearly at the time when we were
in limbo. We were between our first and second *shlichus*. He wished
that we could have had the privilege of the Rebbe telling us personally
and specifically where to go, like when the Rebbe had personal *yechi-
dus* (private discussions with couples) and told them where to go out
on *shlichus*.

My husband then said, "I wish the Rebbe could come to my living
room and discuss the place for me." At the time, it was a difficult thing
to hear. I was silent, for what else could one do for one's spouse when
he was in pain? He wanted to be heard, and one needs to be able to
listen. Being the silent listener to one's spouse is the best way to move
on together with one's *shlichus*, with heart, mind, and soul.

Finally, after many months, I told my husband that somehow, the
Rebbe would send someone to our living room to help us figure out

where to go. At the time, I knew they sounded like sweet, comforting, but unrealistic words. However, it was all that we had in hopes of us going out once again.

Our second position as emissaries would be so much harder to find, and sacrifices would have to be made. Could we handle it? Would we find a place that we both felt was right?

Since I was a little eight-year-old girl, I wanted to go out and build a community from scratch. Yet, my husband preferred to be in an already existing community.

It was like the seesaw of life, wishing we both could stand still in mid-air and succeed in our perception of wrong versus right. Unfortunately, there was only one destination we needed to arrive at, and I strongly disagreed with the idea of an already established place.

After already having been to a larger community the first time around, I thought it should be different the second time. I felt that my husband's personality and ability to communicate easily would be better suited to a community that needed a rabbi. He needed a position where he could roll up his sleeves and be available at late hours of the night.

It was about a year of interviews before our destiny fell into our laps. You know the saying about *zivugim* (life partners): The first match is one's *mazal* (luck), and the second one is according to one's good deeds. To our dismay, the physical comforts were illusory.

There were no restaurants and no school for our children. And it was a two-hour drive to the nearest *mikvah* (a bath used for ritual immersion). This would be harder than what we could have ever imagined, but definitely possible. It just meant that each step forward would take triple the effort.

Sometimes, I like to take a child's approach to a windy path, comparing our obstacles in life to that of a kid. It fascinates me that children can switch from being sad to being happy in a relatively short time.

What changed for the child? His attention was diverted, and now his full focus is on the new moment. Even when there are bumps along the way, the child still stands strong.

The wheels started to turn in the right direction, and after many places that were not for us, we were privileged for the Rebbe's *shliach* to come to our living room and make us part of the team. It was like the Rebbe was saying, "You're not alone here. This is my emissary to take you by the hand and let you be part of the world of emissaries."

I remember that day; it was like floating in a dream. A car pulled up, and a friendly old Jewish man came out and knocked on our door. He had a very long white beard and a great smile.

I was eager to make a whole kitchen full of food. I had missed running around for everyone in need, so I baked up a storm, and shortly afterward, the table was full of bagels, lox, and cakes.

As we were eating, he was surprised that I was so careful not just to serve him but also to plate my husband's food. He then carefully asked me if we were newlyweds. "No," I said shyly. I knew he was surprised but didn't ask again. How could I really explain to this kind and saintly man that this was my way of showing respect and honor to my husband?

Regardless of how little or many years we were married, it was nice to go out of my way to serve him a plate full of food like we were newlyweds each day. Life can be busy or not so busy, but our level of respect shouldn't slide down in the process.

He then proceeded to our living room and had a full *shlichus* meeting with us. He asked us questions in such a gentle but quizzical way that made us want to answer proudly yet be smart and assertive in our answers. When he got up to leave, he was beaming with a kind yet mischievous smile.

His happy persona made us want to laugh and cry all at the same time because the good, hard results of getting the position were standing in the doorway.

So, with just a few short words, a diamond in my living room—the Rebbe's *shliach*—had reignited the candles in our hearts. *Baruch Hashem*, it was very soon afterward that we agreed to get sent out once again.

the letter that saved him from cremation

Words in a letter changed the course of this man's fate.

the sunrise filled a blank canvas, and the day's peace pushed the dark of night aside to welcome the warmth and cheer of morning.

My week, which was regularly filled to the brim without a second's break, was oddly less packed. It was as if there was space for one more event, some time left to help another person in need. Whether dead or alive, each one is under our care, and we must be there to support and help them.

The day was coming to a close; the lights were turned off one by one, and there seemed to be a semblance of harmony and tranquility to the day's gentle end. Strange, one might wonder, our home usually held in its enclave many footsteps, voices, and a small but loud audience. It was an audience that relished our noticing them, adored to be played with, and were excited to be heard.

The tone of a relaxing evening changed suddenly, and the tune and pace dynamically quickened its beat. A rush of anxiety came toppling over the room's serenity. Simultaneously, the keys' typing created a tantrum that fell into a rhythm, a continuous slamming on the desk's surface accompanied by the buzzing and flashing of the phones playing as different messages flew back and forth.

"Are you serious? He passed away! How?" I said, aghast. My voice broke the eerie silence in the room. The silence wasn't there to calm us, but to provoke us into action regarding this new tragedy. In the stillness, our reaction to this newly added grief told a story all its own.

"I just got off the phone with his son, and he passed away very suddenly," my husband told me, looking very solemn as any rabbi would when he just lost a congregant and friend. My husband continued, "They have decided to go through with the cremation. What's worse, his son is pushing very hard for this."

Taking a deep breath and tilting back his chair, my husband retreated inward into his usual thinking mode. He, a skilled problem solver, should be able to fix this, right? Oddly enough, he couldn't solve this travesty, and instead, our hands were tied, and we both were left frustrated and bewildered about what to do.

Clearly giving up on the choice to try to fight and knowing that it was over and there were no straws left to even deal with here, my husband leaned a bit forward and slowly said, "It's a shame because this man's son is only doing what he felt was his father's dying wish." He shook his head solemnly.

"I will call his wife," I said, feeling the pangs of sadness grasp my heart as I knew that I needed to inform her. The widow—my sweet, dear friend—always joined my weekly classes, and my news was about to cause her extreme sadness and distress. Still, I had no choice because she needed me to tell her.

I held my breath, bracing myself to hear her recognition of this sad, devastating truth. Could my soul handle listening to her mourn and watch her unbridled, morbid anguish unfold?

Did it matter what I felt? Whether it did or not, the debate was over! My fingers automatically, with alacrity and quick precision, dialed her number. It shocked me how fast my fingers could move even though I already knew our conversation and its final result.

"No, my kids didn't tell me, and I don't know why they would hide this from me! They probably didn't want me to stop the cremation, and I could, but it would be very hard, and I probably should just let him die with his wish," she said, choking up and starting to cry as one close friend does with another.

I could hear her sorrow and tried to prevent my tears from coming through, but the tears broke free and started pouring down my face. I purposely placed the phone above my cheek so that my voice was forcibly muted for fear of causing her more affliction. After hearing what this man's fate would be, hearing her heartbreak made the pain that much worse.

It would be so hard to save him. Was there even a chance? I felt that she was hanging on by a thread. Will G-d save him? Holding myself together—or what still remained strong regardless of how I felt—I promised to stay in touch.

It was the next day, and a few hours before my *Tanya* class, I decided that I had to try once more to see if there was time. I knew I was pulling on strings that were probably already broken or discarded, but I had to try for this Jewish man.

He needed a Jewish funeral! My voice somehow started spewing out words, stories, teachings of our foremothers and forefathers, not knowing if I made sense, but I knew time was of the essence, and the sand in the hourglass was running out!

After all my gibberish, hoping I made an impact and a difference, my friend, in a regretful tone, said quietly to me, "Well, I think they already cremated him."

I had that falling feeling of knowing you were defeated, and the race was over. This old Jewish man was stuck and could not be helped, and a terrible sin had taken place. I felt that my husband's friend was just sentenced to the electric chair after all his stays in the court procedure were finished. This man was innocent! My voice screamed, but no sound came out.

"Did they tell you?" I mumbled, trying to be gentle and leaving a purposeful, lingering kindness to my tone for fear of obstructing a beautiful friendship.

My friend became more alert and tried to help what seemed like a pointless discussion: "Well, they said they already put him in the urn. Let me see what I can do. Maybe I can at least have them stop it for now, but let me tell you this, it will take a miracle to pull him out of that metal casket."

Patience, patience, patience, I gently chided myself. G-d has a plan, but I had to move fast. Could he still be saved? "So, there is no way we could stop this?" I said in a quiet but quite matter of fact tone.

"I'm not sure, but it will be within the hour. I just got off the phone with the funeral home, and they're desperate to begin." She threw these words out, but you could almost hear the wheels turn as she spoke, and I listened.

"Do you think that you could stop it?" I said, trying to be calm, remembering my friend and congregant just lost her husband, and a certain gentleness was needed even if time was slipping hurriedly through my hands.

"No. I don't think anyone will listen to me. The children, nursing home, friends, and the funeral home all heard that he wanted this cremation. Even though in the end he expressed his desire to have a funeral, in the end it doesn't matter because nothing is in writing."

I closed my eyes and imagined that I held her hand, but as my eyes opened, I realized it was just a wish to do kindness for a dear friend. Instead, I heard her voice tinged with regret and a sense of deep sadness.

"With our son so adamant about having them perform the cremation, it would take a miracle to stop it," she said, sounding upset. She knew she had to recognize that this was fate, and she needed to let go of the struggle to fight.

I got off the phone and looked at my husband, who had just walked into the room. I mouthed the words that we had to at least try, and we both went to finish our classes for the night.

I struggled within myself to do the right thing. What was the right thing to do? Do I still have my *Tanya* class (based on the kabbalistic work written by Schneur Zalman of Liadi in the 1700s) and should I attempt to keep the schedule for the night? Or should I keep pushing this *mitzvah* (commandment) and be there instead for my friend?

The *Tanya* class won out, I realized that I needed to keep to the schedule. Letting others learn Torah was vital, and it would not be fair for me to cancel. Things could wait for an hour because everything was on hold for the night, or I hoped it would be.

I got a phone call after my *Tanya* class, and it was my friend, his widow, and she said excitedly, "I don't know why I did this, but even though I skipped class tonight, I read the *Tanya* letter, and it was all about how even the body is holy and not just the soul. I never knew that. This chapter, this letter of *Tanya*, was speaking to me. I can't just ignore what is right and what is true, and I have to stop the cremation!"

I admired my friend, who wasn't even an observant woman but a nice, Jewish, G-d-fearing person. I felt a warmth light up my half-asleep limbs. "I am so inspired, and I'm very proud of you. It won't be easy, and we will have to move fast! People will try to stop us at every turn, but we still have to be firm in our resolve," I said.

I was trying to be hopeful of convincing her and myself to make the impossible possible as I looked out the window. I stared at the dark sky with the sliver of the white shine of the moon facing me, trying to feel the air and hint of light, but the mood was as cold as the weather. Nothing stirred, and it made me worry more than ever about what was to come.

"So, we want a funeral, but how will I afford it?" She said nervously.

"Stop! Don't think of money. I'll figure it out." I tried to sound confident because I didn't want to dampen her courage or stop her firm resolve to do the right thing. I didn't want her to stop herself from trying to do what was necessary so that her husband would have a kosher and proper Jewish burial.

I wondered how in the world we would find ten thousand dollars, but I dared not reveal this to her. Oy! I had no idea where I would be able to find this type of money, but I would have to because a Jewish man needed a proper burial.

"If you will be willing to help me pay, and your husband agrees, then I will stop the cremation first thing tomorrow morning," she said, relieved and excited that we might have found a way.

"Of course. Money should never be an issue. We will pay for whatever you need," I said, forcing my mind to be clear of worry. My head rushed with this newfound ecstatic wave: we had saved a man from the worst possible fate!

The next morning, I held my overly active breathing. At this point, my pacing began, and the restlessness continued. Does my friend need help? My hands were going back-and-forth messaging again, and

I prayed that I didn't overstep my bounds in being her friend and *rebbetzin*. I should know better and just wait, but I couldn't help myself, knowing that she was hesitant and that the caretaker and their staff were putting pressure on her.

She didn't have proof, or did she? She was legally his wife, but her son, a stubborn Jewish man, felt his way was right, and his way of doing things had to happen, or else. What made it most difficult was that he made his presence at the funeral home known; each minute that ticked by became crucial for my friend to be there, but she just couldn't force herself to go, and therefore her son held the upper hand.

But in the end, she did it! Finally, her messages gave me relief, and it was complete. The papers seemed to fax through on time, and she gave my husband her power of attorney. All the decision-making was settled, and my husband was now in charge. He became the official legal guardian of this man who passed away.

The papers were signed, and now came the next bump in the road: the coffin wouldn't fit. What now? It would be impossible in our small town to find another kosher box, and it would have to be ordered. The son might win, after all!

Finally, my husband called to let me know that they found another kosher box in a warehouse next door that is his size, his Star of David was found, the burial shrouds came in, and all that was left was the *taharah* (purification of the dead).

I told him, "Time is still of the essence; if the son keeps pushing, this could all be turned around."

To my utmost surprise, all I heard on the other side of the phone was laughter, but not the menacing kind. Only relief and excitement flowed and formed into happy notes in my direction.

My husband tried to control his laughter so that he could have a practical conversation with me, but he failed miserably.

He pushed himself to stop laughing and once more continued our discussion, "He changed his mind and wanted a kosher funeral, can you believe it? Now we just need to find a kosher burial plot. Let me see what we can do."

The Jewish people who owned the one last plot in a cemetery nearby that was officially closed during these challenging times agreed. It was a rainy day, but a *minyan* (ten men) was formed, and this old friend, a Jewish synagogue-goer, had a proper kosher funeral. He was ready to go home on his last journey to his Maker.

My friend called me, and her voice sounded angelic and full of life. "Thank you and the rabbi. It was a beautiful funeral. Our decision to bury him instead of having him cremated worked out for the best. I would never have forgiven myself if I chose to let them decide." Her voice trailed off, and I heard her let out a long sigh.

Then her voice grew more assertive and less tired, and she continued, "I know my husband would be happy with my final decision. He needed this, being a part of the Jewish people. The story you told me about the Holocaust and the ovens hit home with me. I know his parents were Holocaust survivors, and this never even should have been an option."

She took another breath, and this time, she was speaking in a higher pitch, but as her voice rose, it stayed full of confidence. I could even hear the hint of her old self finding an entrance. "No Jew deserves to be burned, and that is what cremation is: it is the burning of a holy body, and I couldn't let that happen."

We spoke a bit longer and said goodbye. The next morning my lazy phone buzzed. What could it be, I thought. What was this early rooster call? He already had his burial, and we already spoke late at night. What could have gone wrong?

My friend sounded oddly cheerful. I breathed a sigh of relief. She told me excitedly, "I saw a comet yesterday, and I saw another one this morning! It is definitely a G-dly sign. Do you think it's him? Do you think it's my husband?"

"I know it must be him," I responded, "and G-d is letting us know we did the right thing."

She remained silent, and so did I; we just sat on opposite sides of the phone, resting quietly in each other's company. We were both proud of what we had accomplished and weren't quite ready to hang up the phone.

a soldier under my table

Even when times seem bleak, G-d never leaves us.

the sky turned from day to midnight blue, mixed with toxic dark green. The storm began with a deep tornado hidden in its belly. The sirens rang loud and clear, and the streets became vacant of all humankind.

What would the circumstance turn into? Who would live? Who would die? What life lessons would be handed out to the few, or many, who witnessed tragedy? The answers remain unknown to us—the creations—for the Creator has hidden them deep inside His pockets for safekeeping.

A person from our congregation had gone through a lot of rough patches in life, from a few failed marriages to larger problems at work. He really meant well but thought and reality never seemed to coexist.

They were like two different right hands, never taking the time to meet. It was his last chance to succeed, and we were willing to give him a steady helping hand to hold onto.

A knock at the door set us up to meet this reality, and we went to greet an important guest. We opened the door, and its loud creaking was accompanied by the thumping of sturdy army boots.

A trail of mud quickly appeared on our freshly washed floors. The smell of the outdoors and the army uniform was such that it took us into the officer's world. He was an officer from the National Guard here to interview one of our congregants.

Each congregant is quite different from the other, but they come to Chabad to pray, learn, and bring the traditions of old into their fast-moving lives. For this particular congregant, we had spent extra hours helping him find what he was truly searching for.

He felt torn among the in-betweens of finding the right path and place for him. He struggled with utter exhaustion to make a final decision, but most of all, he wanted his dedicated choice to add new spice and excitement to his life.

I decided to go all out with this guest and presented a family ambiance with a large dinner that felt like coming home. We then ritually washed our hands according to the tradition and helped ourselves to the mountains of good food.

In just a short while, there were smiles and laughter that couldn't be swallowed up in the largest of rooms. The questions kept on rolling: the whys and hows and what ifs of this new expedition. It's not every day that you get to hear such tales.

In the middle of his stories of battle and honor came the sirens for the tornado warning. The sky turned green with a vengeance, a color which locals knew too well—the color that told us what was coming. However, we were out-of-towners and had no clue about the siren or the warning it held.

The officer looked at all of us in shock and disbelief and said, "Quickly, we must go under the table!" He was holding his breath, waiting for us to follow, but all he got was our blank stares of incomprehension.

We pulled out our chairs and just stared at this huge officer under our table; he was hiding there like a four-year-old child and waiting for us to come and follow him as if his clubhouse was there.

He jumped out from under the table, and quickly checked the sky to see if the tornado was picking up, but it didn't, so he then taught us the drills of what to expect with a tornado in your backyard.

All I could think of was that this was a definite *shlichus* moment, a moment where one finds himself in the elements of the unknown, and then is forced into the new reality involved with settling down in the middle of nowhere.

The place where the teacher settles marks the end of an abandoned community. I stood in my own imaginings and hopes for the community.

I cleared the table, and the house once again became quiet, resetting itself for the next visitor in need.

It happened shortly after our current wanderer joined the National Guard that he felt it didn't carry his tune. Our hearts slumped over this man's troubles. His short time in limbo was tough, and we made sure to invite him often.

He missed his children and saw them only on rare occasions because of his troubled marriages, with his latest wife having sent the mob after him. As strange and horrific that this seems, this was this nice man's new existence: survival through difficult moments in time.

Since children are the best medicine for sadness, it did him wonders each time he visited. So, each passing Shabbos he would arrive, and within moments would have the kids bouncing on his knees.

He was like the Shabbos fairy dust, and by the time he left, he had a big smile on his face and a purpose to his walk. After a while, he found work again in another city. We began to get busy with other people in need of our help. It happened unexpectedly, but on Shabbos, out of the blue, he arrived with great news.

It was the right choice for this man who decided not to be in the National Guard, for he was in love again and engaged to be married. This time, though, was different from the other moments of survival that he chose for himself.

This time, he found someone who was the gentlest of persons and knew how to help her troubled husband discover peace and contentment in their life together. Our happiness for him knew no bounds, and as one door closes, another chapter finally opens.

freedom from responsibility

What is true freedom?

We play with the idea of what real freedom is. How lucky is the person who remembers the great lessons he has learned in life. To leave Egypt, the prisons of today, we must remove the chains we place inside ourselves.

One Friday night, as I cleaned and cleared the table after the meal, I noticed a helpful young man. I asked him, "Is your family coming from Israel soon?"

He said, "Yes, I'm very excited for you to meet my wife and family." A few weeks later, I met a lovely young mother with a couple of cute kids.

After settling into our community, it became obvious to the onlooker, let alone one involved, that this man's wife was withdrawn, aloof, and distant from the rest of her family. To be fair, she was feeding off a secular, atheist approach, which portrays that what's right is wrong, and what's wrong is right.

It's the most heartbreaking thing to watch as this couple disregarded one of the keys to having peace in one's home. It became the parents' excuse to hold their arguments in jumbled piles of I, instead of focusing on the bigger picture. It hurt me to watch them, as I took the front row seat to the couple's crowded circles of him vs. her, where the concept of a family unit was forgotten. So, it ended up that every two weeks she toyed with the idea of divorce—today, yes, or no, or maybe.

Her husband had no choice but to go along with her theatrics. If only life were so simple, and we could reclaim the moment that a bad seed was planted in a good person's conscience.

I started learning together with her, as a one-on-one *chavrusa* (study-partner). It went well for a while, and then she decided that she needed a break. In the interim, every possible scenario went through my mind. Would she ever come back to the synagogue?

What would happen if she decided to take a break from Jewish life? It's the chessboard of worry that emissaries know too well, and you feel that if you make one wrong move, a family could be destroyed forever.

It was the cheesecake holiday of Shavuos. After months of her not showing up, I was finally graced with her presence. It's a bittersweet moment: that feeling of missing a long-lost friend with the emotion that mellowed with time.

My thoughts were caught in a wrestling match with one another as the added concerns piled up higher than ever. Each one of my thoughts went off and started popping in its own direction. How would she react? Is she still happy with G-d, or is He in the time-out corner again? Was she still an atheist, or does Hashem have a place in her home?

While I was schmoozing with her, testing gently and feeling out the waters, she pointed out my silly costume, to my utter dismay. She said in a very quizzical tone, "What is the spiritual significance of your shoes?"

I looked down and wanted to hide. In my haste to get everything done, I had put on two completely different black shoes. I was relieved that they looked similar enough that no one else noticed, or perhaps they did and had the best Shavuos ever.

Regardless of the entertainment, my thoughts still found their way to worry over this lost, *frum* (observant in the faith) family. Unfortunately, as emissaries, we can get involved only as deeply as people let us in. It's not our place to pressure her to remain observant or for her to have a close connection to G-d. That is between her and G-d.

The choice ultimately is up to her to make, and I as her *rebbitzin* and friend sometimes must take a step back and allow my congregant to be able to make that choice. Perhaps one can get lucky and break through the glass ceiling which entraps us. We then can encourage them both to continue on a true Torah path as much as possible. We are also there to advise them if they want; or else, to remain on the sidelines to pick up the pieces when they fall.

It's a lesson to be learned—that even if people are more observant, they still need our help. We always hear the expression "learning never ends," and that means here as well, even if we too are meant to learn a hard lesson. It was hard for me to see a *frum* girl accepting atheism and not connecting with Hashem.

strangers in
my backyard

Is it the little angels running around us that
shield us from complete chaos?

footsteps: slow footsteps and the pace quickens, fast footsteps
and then the pace quickens some more—walking, sliding, pushing,
shoving through the race. Will a winner be chosen?

Each Friday night, I walk alone or with one of my small children.
I choose to come later to create a peaceful and warm atmosphere for
the Friday night service.

I always come to the Chabad house a drop late, only after ensuring
everything and everyone has what they need. Six boys jump into their
Shabbos clothes, and the timer of hectic speed begins. Before the boys
and the rabbi head out, I see to it that all is done and children's coats
are buttoned. I then fix what I need to before heading out to join the
community.

It was dark, and I saw a stranger approach closer to me than was normal; I made sure that he passed us while holding on to my little son's
hand. I shrugged it off and thought nothing of it as I crossed over to the
other side of the street.

I then came to the block where I had to cross over with my toddler to
the Chabad house, and as we did, the stranger crossed back over to our
side. When I saw this, I felt it was a bit odd, and it definitely made me
feel a bit nervous.

In my haste to help my children and make a Shabbos atmosphere for my sons, husband, and community, I forgot my safety, and I forgot about being alone. It was just my toddler by my side and me, heavily pregnant, walking alone on a Friday night.

With quickened footsteps, I urged myself and my child to go faster so we would be safe. I then opened the sanctuary doors and entered into a haven for my little son and me. I was welcomed with hugs and kisses from my children and guests, and all of my worries were forgotten.

Sitting down with the guests at the Shabbos table for the meal, I had a minute to think about my day. It was a long one, and it started the night before, Thursday night, in which I spent the time cooking until the wee hours of the morning.

I needed to take care of someone who had passed away, and I took a short rest and then was up bright and early for the great *mitzvah* of purifying the deceased: a job no one asks for and yet no one dares to refuse if asked. After a few hours of cleaning, praying, purifying, and dressing the *mes* (deceased) in shrouds, the task was done.

I went to finish the large job of getting Shabbos ready in time. Everything was finally ready, and we had a beautiful Shabbos meal with many guests from many different backgrounds. It was inspiring and uplifting!

After our Shabbos meal, I put my kids to bed and then rinsed all the dishes. I started to feel overwhelmed that I had not seen any open miracles that day—especially when I went outside my own comfort zone.

Why did I have to see a stranger that night who scared my little son and me? I wanted *Hashem* (G-d) to make special miracles just for me. It's what every woman wants, especially when we feel a bit tired, drained, and underappreciated at times.

That night I fell asleep, and I had a very eye-opening dream. I was in a house that looked like a bunker with my kids. It was literally in the middle of nowhere. It was getting dark, and my husband was not yet back from teaching his classes.

I called once and left a message asking when he would be home. Then came the waiting and having patience for him to arrive home. As I hung up the phone, I saw what appeared to be a reflection of a person in my backyard. I felt confused and then frightened. What was a stranger doing in my backyard?

I peered out the window once more to get a better look at the reflection from the yard, and no longer was a stranger standing there, but a lone soldier. I looked closer and saw that he was not alone but had brought company.

Soon enough, there was a knock on my door, and I heard the words, "*Shalom, Rabbanit* (*Rebbetzin* for Israeli Jews), can we come in?" I heaved a sigh of relief when I saw that somehow these soldiers were Jewish, friendly, and wanted to come to us.

I quickly unlocked the door, and they rushed to play with my children. The children were laughing and shrieking and begging for it to be their turn to play. The kids looked happy, and the soldiers looked even happier—if that was possible.

The doorbell kept ringing, and more and more soldiers came to play with the children, and each time one slipped inside my protective seal on the door. As they slipped in, there were always the whispered tunes of "Thank you, *Rabbanit*, for letting me inside to play with the kids."

The door kept swinging every few seconds, and I began to feel overwhelmed. I was still trying to figure out what was going on before letting the entire army into my tiny little home.

I asked them, "So why are you here, of all places? Shouldn't you be at your army post?"

They answered me, while still playing with the children, "We came to protect you and your post: it is far away and a difficult one at that. We are always here, and now is the first time that you have seen us."

When I woke up, I sat there for a few minutes before my bed was covered with kids who wanted hugs and help getting dressed. I slid into my fast-paced morning routine but wondered to myself, what was the meaning of this strange dream?

As the day got busy, I started running around to complete the day's marathon. The dream nagged at back of my head like a mosquito. I then thought about it some more, and I realized that's how we think that big miracles have to happen. If we don't see G-d, that doesn't mean he is not holding us upright in challenging times.

The soldiers: maybe that's how the *malachim* (angels) appeared, as our protectors, who are always there helping us and are sent as messengers to make things easier.

When it is so hard, and especially on long nights on *shlichus* when the rabbi is away helping everyone, who is helping me?

The kids seem to make it to bed okay, things seem to straighten out, and the night classes seem to get done. Is it the little angels running around us that shield us from complete chaos?

Maybe, probably, and even if we are alone with no angels, it's nice to imagine that they are there to help us over the hurdles in our good, chaos-filled life.

Dreams: What do they tell us? Some are silly, and some can be scary, and some give us courage for the next day's events. These images are kept in the deep recesses of the mind and are only expressed during sleep. Perhaps they give us the strength to understand different occurrences that happen into our day-to-day living.

I like to imagine each *shlucha* (a women emissary) or *shliach* (a man emissary) who is away doing a mission as being protected; protected from outside forces that can hurt the spiritual sanctuary each day being built. It's not just at work but also in everyday family life. We then have the *koach* (strength) to keep putting one more positive day into growing the next generation.

the tagalong critic

If we open our hearts and minds to others,
usually good things will come of it.

in the dance with time to get out the food—with all the sweat and hopes for success that it entails—the room of smiles also contains the stares of a few critics. The critic: the first to laugh at the hint of failure and the last to admit your success. You wonder: Why do the critics come? What's in it for them?

Perhaps they, too, want to be truly impressed and truly accepted, even if they are throwing a tantrum! The critics and even the tagalong critics want unconditional support, love, friendship, and kindness.

When we are at our post, our public needs are filled with the fans and the critics. It happened when I was greeting each guest that came as the *rebbetzin* (rabbi's wife) of the community, that I bumped into the biggest of critics.

Her permanent frown and constant criticism cued me into her life, values, and goals. Here she was, lost and confused, a person looking for real truth but scared to change her views on what truth really is.

Year after year, she brought the same growl of hello and short good-byes. Everything seemed wrong: from the tasty food to the perfectly placed cutlery. It always seemed like the complaints arrived just for the sake of arriving. Whenever I saw her, I began to expect her complaints, her patience getting shorter, and my kids bumping into her. She seemed to abhor them more and more each time she visited.

Soon she began to come more often, and it was *Seder* (first meal of Passover) night. That year we had sixty people the first night, and she was our only guest the second night. The fireworks of her critiques came in a vengeful tone and could not be calmed. Children, noise, and on and on, the critique exploded. It was past midnight, and she decided to leave when suddenly she burst into a fit of rage against me with my children clinging to my skirt. I bravely and humbly wished her well and said good night.

However, it did bother me—her tone and inability to stop judging us and forgo making groups, critiques, and divisions in Judaism. If I cared about divisions, then I wouldn't be on *shlichus* helping all kinds of Jews.

There was no point in addressing this issue because I knew she wasn't ready to hear critique even if she liked to give it to others. I pushed those unwanted thoughts from my head and kept trying to focus on doing what is right.

After Pesach, I started to receive emails from her. She sent one email and then two; she, the critic, was afraid of not being invited again! That whole concept felt silly to me, and I emailed her back. I told her that at Chabad, she is always welcome and that we are looking forward to seeing her for Lag B'Omer (the thirty-third day of the Omer).

The holidays flew by so fast they almost knocked each other over like a deck of cards, but this time the critic was different. This time she had a bounce in her step; still a critic, complaining to her drum about everything that was wrong, but less mean. The critique was more and more accompanied by smiles, as she reluctantly embraced this new positivity as her own.

Time went on, it was one of those snowy nights, and again I bumped into the critic. We met again at our common friend's house, and I, usually unsure of her mood, found myself holding in my breath as a habit and waiting for the storm.

Would there be one? What was in store for me? Was the whirlwind of a disaster tornado coming to knock me over and then apologize? First encounters after a while with my critic friend made me feel uneasy.

The shock came fast—hurriedly from an unexpected corner she came and embraced me. "*Rebbetzin*, I'm so glad to see you!" she said.

I quickly checked to see, perhaps at this small party there was another *rebbetzin* I was missing. When I realized that she meant me, I said, "You are?"

I quickly turned on my loving, adoring warmth of a smile, even though I felt a bit nervous. As a congregant and a daughter of Israel, she always deserved my love and warmth, even if I felt that sometimes it was not always reciprocated.

"Yes! I am," she said, more relaxed than usual with a hint of a smile on the corners of her lips. "I need to tell you something. Can you follow me?"

"Sure," I said, almost sounding scared and really glum. I tried to think positive thoughts, but my head kept taking me to a place on my own with the critic, and that image froze any whispers of light that tried to seep in.

When we came to an abandoned corridor, she looked me up and down and said, "Can I trust you?"

My heart started jumping, and my head felt it would fall in. What is she talking about? First, I have to follow her, and now she doesn't want to talk to me? I looked at her again, and I was glad that she couldn't read my thoughts and said, "Of course you can trust me."

I understood that she felt worried, but she shouldn't feel that I would betray her. I never share other people's stories once they share them with me. It is between them and me, and I tried to make sure each shared message stays locked in a chest of silence where no movement of words comes out.

She whispered to me that she had cancer and was suffering. I looked up at her again, but this time, gone were my nerves and the feeling of dread about what the critic can say to me. I embraced her and held her tight as the dearest friend that I hadn't seen in months.

She said that it was caught early, and she, with G-d's help, was given a good chance of survival. We slowly walked out of our secret corridor, and it felt strange to be with her and stepping into the crowd's regular light.

The next time we met, our embrace felt more natural and less gruff. She seemed like an old friend to me, even if to the untrained eye, she still sounded like a rottweiler whose treat you just stole. She was still my congregant, and I began to feel more protective of her and less on guard to how she came off in general. I realized each gem is packaged differently, but in *Hashem's* (G-d's) eyes, we are all His diamonds. As an emissary, I needed to consider that perspective as my own.

I don't know where the change within her came from, but it was embraced by many. She is still the critic, and she often whispers with disapproval and fireworks full of revenge.

Although this time around, the fireworks are quieter and the revenge less harsh. Perhaps it's a good sign, for when one embraces all with love and kindness, it's usually felt and reciprocated. A real effort rarely goes unnoticed, and rarely ever does its imprint become erased.

After her story unfolded, it became much clearer that we really don't know one another as much as we think we do. One kind word or one good deed can change the world and better us as a people.

a friend's request

One needs to go outside one's comfort zone
to help a friend in need.

an older woman who seemed so sure of herself, so real in her faith, so full of truth and essence, had drawn me in to be her friend. We hit it off, regardless of her age, and became close.

After spending plenty of Shabbosim together, it became apparent that her unwillingness to be gentle to people who disagreed with her was a problem. I tried to gently tell this grandmother to be a little less harsh and a little more mild, but she refused and took my words as the ultimate betrayal.

I could feel the room brewing and the effect of an explosive situation that had already transformed into a big but silent argument. The tension could have been sliced into thirds with a machete, and still no crease would have been seen.

Sometimes, it feels much better to be involved in a loud argument than a silent, tiptoeing one. One may assume that these arguments are just silly, but the truth is that a quiet but powerful disagreement can be much worse than a traditional noisy one. One could imagine a silent argument where each stands off, guns at the ready, but no noise is heard.

"How long have they been outside?" I wondered aloud, looking straight at my husband, whose head was turned to face the outdoors, and the rest of him was half-hidden in the curtains of the Chabad house.

My husband took his eyes off the window for a split second to look at me, and to do so, he had to fumble through the curtains. When he could finally see me, he said, "Well, probably an hour, maybe two."

I couldn't believe that we found ourselves in what appeared to be a game with teams, not of mine or my husband's choice, but as something thrown upon us: this tantrum from a woman I truly respected.

The argument of silence put me in a daze in which I had the forlorn feeling of being left holding the bag. It was a bag full of this newfound realization that I was closed outside her circle of warmth and friendship. A friendship that I admired and adored was now locked and bolted forever.

Instead, I felt a freezing, cold, piercing breeze of my new reality in which I found myself standing behind the stubborn door of an argument that did not pass over with time.

Every once in a while, dagger eyes stared at us, and we wanted to hide somewhere, but no place seemed safe enough. Instead, we stood like small little children in the curtains of our great Chabad house and waited worriedly for her return.

The phone calls stopped playing their tune, and the Chabad house felt emptier without her, but I knew that this choice was right. The community couldn't be thrown in a constant time-out just because someone slighted her. I had to speak up, and that meant losing a friendship that I had cherished.

A short time passed, the phone rang, and we fell limp to our chairs. Her daughter had passed away in the middle of the night. Could I supervise the *taharah* (purification of the dead)?

It was like a double-edged sword. How could I take care of a *mes* (deceased person)? What should I tell her? No? The "no" word would never be right; it would never be real for me to utter such a word, so I said with my nerves in my throat, "Of course, it would be my honor."

It was my friend's request, and I could not refuse, no matter how much discomfort it caused me. It had to be done, and I had to be the one to do it.

I had a short time to prepare, and being my first *taharah*, I frantically called as many teachers as I could find. *Baruch Hashem* (Blessed is G-d), I was lucky in my choice, and I had the privilege of finding a woman who really knew the laws well and was a master of presentation. Feeling a bit more confident, I felt the time was right to proceed.

As I came to the home of the dead, I saw a group already there and felt that they were very much in their element. The only problem was the *taharah* was being done in a way which was worse than a *bedieved* (a position forced from circumstance). Such a young woman—who would fight for her, if not me?

My mind began playing the game of truth versus politeness, and truth won out. I kindly said, "Let's pour more water on her." The stares and laughs that I got were enough to feel smaller than the shoes on my feet.

However, it didn't perturb me, for something had to stall them for a true and real *taharah*, but what could it be? It happened suddenly: my break happened, and the *mes* herself started vomiting, which was Divine providence because it is so rare, and it was my cue to suggest a brand new *taharah*.

She then was wrapped with love in her shrouds, prayed over, and gently placed in her eternal resting place. The door to her box was closed, and we lit her candle and left. I felt sad for her passing but happy for a chance to do it right.

My husband and I then had to go to the funeral and participate in her burial. It was the hardest thing that I've ever had to do. I had to stand and comfort a mother who lost her only daughter forever and a grieving friend who would never find true comfort ever again.

Her sobbing and screaming shook the cemetery from its silence; there were no dry eyes, and many cried with her, including me. The dirt was poured, and the coffin was lowered into the earth. Her little grandchildren are now without their mother and have lost a companion forever.

Her husband, their grandfather, was holding their hands and was white as a sheet. He tried pacing to at least do something, but in reality, he knew the battle was over. She, his only daughter, was being lowered into the ground forever.

After a while, I walked to the fence where an old man greeted me: "Congratulations! I heard you are now part of the club. It's not an easy job, but an undeniably tough one."

I then asked this kind old man, "How do you do it, a *taharah* for friends and family, and handle such a task? How, after everything that's done, can you grieve with those who lost loved ones?"

"It gets easier," he said, "but it's hard. That's part of the job. We don't choose the job, but the job chooses us."

It's not always what's comfortable in life, but it's what's necessary to fulfill what G-d really demands of a person. Even if that means getting comfortable with what's uncomfortable in one's own self, when this goal is your focus, then the details won't seem that important anymore.

After that day, the task got easier because my focus was in the right place. My heart cared and wanted to do the *mitzvah* (commandment) right, and the little details didn't seem to matter anymore.

the great fire on shabbos

A person is a miniature world.

shabbos was here! Each Shabbos we dedicate to our community, and not once do we even imagine taking a vacation. With our lifelong commitment of love and loyalty, we stay in our shul and help those in need. Instead of getting annoyed or overwhelmed, we focus ourselves each day on what more we can do with even greater zeal than the day before.

One may wonder why we picked ourselves up, out of our own Chabad community, to come to serve others, where each day that we serve our community is so much more about giving with less, and less about taking. What is in it for us? Why do we spend so much effort even to help one single Jew who is not usually observant in smaller towns?

We are Chabad: it becomes like the air we breathe to help a fellow in need. We even beg to go out to communities so bereft of anything Jewish just to help our brethren excel in their observance of Torah and *mitzvos* (commandments).

In the community that my husband and I were gifted, there was no *minyan* (a group of ten men), no kosher store, no *mikvah* (a bathhouse for spiritual purity), and no school. Instead, there was lots of resistance all the way around. The cold weather meddled with our daily hard efforts to warm up the Frozen Tundra.

Even when it wasn't on the weather radar, lots of cold, ice, and snow were tossed on each block as a sign of resistance to our hard efforts.

Nevertheless, we were thrilled to help out each person in need. Our sleeves were rolled up, and we eagerly put in the sweat of our brow to help it thrive.

It seemed on this particular Shabbos that our three regular tables were fast becoming overcrowded with guests, which is a great feeling for one who loves to serve and give to others; the more, the merrier, I thought. A fourth table was pulled out, and we all heard the *kiddush* (the blessing ceremony over the wine on Friday night and Shabbos morning) and the blessings over the bread.

Once filled with so much food, the table was quickly in its own magic act as the food was disappearing!

A million questions seemed to fly in my direction as my kids forgot their chairs and made their way over to my already filled lap. I usually didn't mind feeling like the football and having five kids on my lap, but my concentration was beginning to buckle. I wanted each congregant wanting my attention to be heard!

Finally, I served the soup and had a few helpers who already made their way downstairs. I realized my mistake as quickly as I came down: I forgot to remind them about the *blech* (a metal plate that goes over the fire used on Shabbos) and how we serve food on Shabbos.

It was all too late! A fire had broken out on Shabbos. The flames were jumping all over the place, and I felt that the air was becoming too thick and hard to breathe. The kitchen looked like a scene from a bad picture book with no firefighters at the ready. It was Shabbos, and I had to move fast!

I had to focus my mind at a hurried pace: the *blech* was on fire, a foot above where it should be. I realized how much and how fast fire feeds on plastic bowls.

One minute soup was being served in a relaxed, calm, and happy atmosphere, an atmosphere where kitchen secrets, laughter, and wholesomeness spreads its warmth.

A minute later, I heard, "Oh, no! What happened? There was a fire under that? What is that, some kind of burner?" My guest first muttered, then screamed.

All I could think of was the children who were playing near the kitchen. We have to get everyone to a safe place, and then make sure that my guest's feelings won't be hurt. The guest can't feel broken after this experience. I just shook my head; it was all too much.

I sent everyone upstairs and asked the troops to come down. My husband and three other Israelis came down and worked fast to figure out an appropriate way to keep the Shabbos while not letting the Chabad house burn to the ground.

I thought my husband would stand with me in the doorway and let the Israelis take over. After all, they were all in the army, but to my surprise, he fearlessly picked up the *blech* with fire two feet above it now and gently put it in the sink.

The fire slowly put itself out in the metal sink. We all looked around, and the first words I heard were laughter and then, "You did a good job! Let me guess; this wasn't your handiwork?" My husband, with his humor, made the rest of the helpers laugh and feel more relaxed.

"I'm not going to answer that because we have company, and it doesn't matter anyway. Everyone is OK," I said, still in shock and not yet ready for humor. I continued, "It is crucial that we just open the windows and the door upstairs. We should just act like everything is normal and nothing happened."

The troops all shook their heads at me, then one brave helper said, "C'mon, Rabbanit, maybe that person should be more careful. How can we pretend nothing happened? Look around you; there is still smoke in the air with plastic bowls swirling."

As we all started to go upstairs, I was so thankful that the air conditioner was on and the windows were open to give us some good ventilation. In a low voice, I still told some of the men who would be sleeping over that they could crash at our home if they needed to.

Meanwhile, upstairs my kids and some of their friends were doing cartwheels and somersaults outside. I heard myself say, "Are you done playing? Can we go back to our Shabbos meal?"

"Oh, we're still having a meal? I mean, I thought our Chabad house building would burn to the ground!" my eight-year-old said, looking frightened, but at the same time, he seemed to be having fun.

The guest, my friend, kept feeling awful, but I just kept changing the topic, worried that she might blame herself and never return. She was making great progress in her journey and was dedicating Friday nights to learning more about Judaism. How could I take this beautiful experience from her?

I served the rest of the meal, and the next morning no one even noticed anything out of place. After years of fundraising and even donating money out of our own pocket to buy this beautiful building, I was so thankful that everything was OK. If it were simply destroyed, that would have been beyond devastating for me.

I was glad that everything turned out well, but unfortunately, the guest was very embarrassed to come back, and it took about six months for her to return. After she eventually returned, she became a regular again but with more passion about coming each Friday night.

It seems like everything and everyone turned out to be safe and well. However, a few minor changes were made. I made the rule that I always serve the soup, and I am the first person to go down the stairs and the last one to go up the stairs.

I realized one is never truly alone. Hashem (G-d) has mysterious ways of protecting us from great harm. I forever remain thankful and indebted to Hashem that He saved us from the Great Fire on Shabbos!

the chicken or the egg

It's the age-old question: Which comes first, the chicken or the egg? When does a good seed turn into a badly broken one, or a bad seed blossom into a newly recharged good one?

light and goodness was pouring in from all directions. Even as nightfall came, the flow from the sun just kept on overstaying its welcome. The moon became impatient with his disobedient friend, but the sun persevered and victoriously stood there for this most memorable occasion.

Our little old Chabad house just seemed to bask in all the attention. It seemed almost subconsciously that one would tune in to the whisperings of music that could be heard as the clitter-clatter of plates bounced on top of the tables.

Just a few moments passed, and this holiday began to pick up steam with people pouring in from all around town. Cars honking, Jewish people celebrating that was reflected everywhere, and the doorbell played its own instrument: ping pong on the bell. No need to wonder about the chaos; it's just *Pesach* (Passover) once again.

There were expected visitors, friends that we were familiar with since the beginning of our time here. They came to celebrate freedom but faithfully held onto the traditions of old. The hardship and difficulty for them was that their only little girl was finding her way in life, barren of the wells of Torah.

What comes naturally to the regular Jewish kid found no standing with their only daughter. She was now a young teenager and in love with a nice non-Jewish boy. Like a precious gem handed to a curious toddler, it would take just a moment of neglect until all that's left of over a 3,000-year legacy is lost forever.

When there is a child, teen, or even an adult who seems to have lost his or her way, we sometimes ponder this curious question: Is it the rooster's fault, the chicken, or the egg?

The parents felt a lot of frustration, anguish and grief, wanting to undo what was done, to be able to reset the wheel to turn right rather than left.

How can time be stopped and re-set to create a perfect world? Unfortunately, it cannot; they came to us, their *shluchim*, at the end of their rope, which had become torn and faded.

It felt the contrast in our *heimishe* house. On the one hand, the *Pesach* flavor and family atmosphere seemed to sparkle and circulate a peaceful togetherness as a close-knit community.

On the other hand, frantic, nervous friends—worried about the future of their last family member—created a deep concern and hopelessness in our hearts. Perhaps, there was no such thing as contrast at all, for this is the true idea of Pesach (Passover). On Pesach, it becomes about the Haggadah and the *mitzvah* of telling the story to one's children—having an impact on one's family, and their future.

A short while later, we began the *Seder* (the Passover meal), with people from all walks of life eagerly participating and sharing. Amongst the mayhem, time felt of the essence, and in the middle of the *seudah* (holiday meal), we found time to have a chat with the young lady herself.

We spoke about life and other things, but the main point portrayed was love and a sense of responsibility. As an only child, she inherited the future generations on her sleeve, and it was up to her to take responsibility to be the tomorrow for her past of forebears.

Time flew by, and the girl went to college. Now, college can be a place of serious change, and most *shluchim* hold their breath for it to be a positive one. One day, she came into the Chabad house with a skirt touching the floor and a smile that reflected the happiness of one that found the ultimate truth.

Well, you can only imagine her parents' whispered devastation. There was a deep silence of sorts that came over them with fresh tears on their faces to place into a bottle of what could have been. I'm not sure which was worse for them, their daughter losing her Jewish identity or her decision to become more observant.

It was a decision that wrecked years of meticulous planning of a secularized future to be grasped. In our friends' way of thinking, a secular career with a tad of tradition was the only way they could envision purpose and accomplishment in life; anything but that was devastating.

Sometimes, the Jewish tradition of old is put as a trophy in one's pocket for safekeeping, but one never really invests in its work. I should have taken ten steps back, but the nagging of my soul pushed me to move on forward and make the Rebbe proud. After many tearful days, she turned the page and is now observant.

Time moves on, and I started learning more seriously with this new *baalas teshuvah* (a woman who becomes observant in the faith). She instinctively put her new learnings into practice and strongly persevered through many tearful and sorrow-filled nights. Her parents, with time, became accustomed to her new lifestyle and reluctantly embraced her.

We were the lucky ones and had the privilege to get the exciting news that she was about to get engaged. The red rose scent that scurried through the air spread over all of us.

So, it now seems, with over a decade of soul searching one finds truth, and an acceptance has arrived at this family's doorstep. Her parents seem filled with bliss, and as one door opens, another one finally closes.

the guilty verdict

We felt terrible, but justice was served.

When one thinks of a villain, they're usually depicted in plays or films as the big-bad-monster. The faceless monster always has the same common garb of evil, which is noticed wherever he goes, and he commonly leaves behind him a trail of tears and misery.

What happens when this monster is disguised as a regular, nice, honest person who has a severe problem that leads to a terrible mistake? It's these people who remain unnoticed until it's too late for them, but also too late for the ones who have been deeply hurt and affected by their selfish actions.

A friend, father, mother, wife, brother, sister—all share in the shame. Who is it hardest for, one might ask? It's the hardest for one's mother and also one's rabbi. One can wonder, a rabbi so affected and saddened by his pupil? Yes, even the simplest of people can have a profound influence on a rabbi, as he touches souls for a living, and his own soul is affected by things such as an ugly truth.

It was a regular Friday night, and my kids were each caught on full display practicing to be little rabbis. In walks the typical, semi-observant Shabbos keeper. He had a warm smile, a nice handshake, and a certain over-politeness about him.

I was on the other side of the room, where the kids were whining, the table was not yet set, and the food still had to be plated. He was quick to get everything done before you had even to ask. It was such a breeze to have such help and to have such company.

The one-on-one learning for a Torah *shiur* (class) began, and he became a real regular each Friday night.

Trickle, trickle, trickle, and news started to come our way. This shul, that shul, and another shul all closed their doors to him. Why? What were we missing? What was the disconnect?

My husband soon found out some news, but it was bits and pieces of half a hidden story. We heard that there would be a verdict, and then we would have our answers. So we decided to wait for his day of judgment patiently. At least we knew for now that his misdeed couldn't hurt the broader family of our community.

Seder (the Passover meal) night came flying in, and he came to help out. This nice, polite, graying man who had a court case hanging over his head shrugged off the obvious and brought his children along, now young adults. Each one of them was close to him—the man with a hidden story.

It was a unique treasure for him and a very noticeable pat on the back that his kids were close and connected to him. Perhaps for him, it was just luck, or maybe he was doing his part as a good father.

However, this moment of recognition is overshadowed by his insecurity and the overwhelming need to prove his side of a glass half full. Instead, that whole evening when he helped us at the *Seder* only brought a thick cloud of selfish fog.

He had this want, desire, and need to be right; this became his obsession the whole night long. He tediously and cowardly tried to keep bringing up his side of the glass half full, his story and not the overall picture of what really happened. He wanted to paint himself in a favorable light.

No one wanted to be a part of this story, and I didn't want to drag myself into it, on account that I, too, didn't like to voice my opinion.

It was something that I saved for my husband's ears only, his trusted rabbi, who was a good listener and whose opinion had real weighted worth. Leaving it to my husband, the rabbi, was especially helpful in putting this man's tale of wrongdoing into proper perspective.

As long as my children and congregants were safe, that was the paramount peace for me because I, too, cared for souls that came knocking on my door. I felt that peace needed to be my calling as a *rebbetzin*; peace always stood by me as my all-time friend in all my hours of need.

In general, I would rather keep a distance from gossip than know each unpleasant situation that hides inside my congregants' shoes. It is a good, positive, arms-length that gives my congregants enough space and allows me not to be too overbearing. This, I feel, builds the connection between a *rebbetzin* and her congregation.

My approach always let my congregants have space, so being overly involved in this man's hidden story bothered me. I didn't want my mind to wander and taint my own imaginings to an unknown tale of him and his half a glass.

All of a sudden, without my consent, I felt dragged into his story. He started crying, and it was like heavy darts were being thrown at me, and nothing missed—one after another, after another, and some more after that! A grown man crying in my kitchen! What was I to do?

He looked up, stopped crying, and then wanted to know what I thought. What was my view? Instead of taking the bait, I tried to keep the conversation short.

I saw his emotional discomfort and deep pain, but I also knew that there are two sides to every happening and circumstance. There was a noticeable absence in the room for me, and that was the one person who wasn't able to share his side of this tragedy.

As much suffering and finger-pointing that this man felt he needed to express, I understood that someone else was also just as saddened and terribly hurt. I tried to keep the conversation short and asked that he review the many details of his case with my husband, and if he needed anything else, I would try to help.

Uh-oh! I held my breath and felt the inevitable happen. The community started to get involved, and my kids started to get used to his presence at the Shabbos table. Time did not stop because we cared. The date of this verdict moved closer and finally came.

Both sides were heard, and the judge announced his earth-shattering decision: it was six months in jail for this man's misdeed. A once super-polite man will be forgotten, and he will have time to reflect on his moment of selfishness. There is always way more to the story than meets the eye. In a Chabad house where everyone is always welcome, sometimes one meets a person from within the community who did something wrong.

Sometimes, one needs to be removed from his broader Jewish family, even where there is always a Jewish house for everyone to thrive, a *shul*, a Chabad center, and a place to call home. However, a deeper need must be met to protect our congregants, family, and friends.

So, each decision one makes has its particular impact on where it falls. It might mean that one has regrettably chosen to bring his fate outside his family, his community, and his shul.

I felt bad for him and his punishment, but he will learn a hard lesson! However, I felt more upset about the terrible, selfish decision that caused a good father, a good friend, and a well-mannered person to be brought down by one act of wrongdoing. Justice was served, and a guilty man was sentenced.

the kitchen boss

A quiet voice, with a kind heart, and a will
to turn over each corner, is the real deal.

it was a time of celebration, a time of joy, and an invitation to share
in happiness for a *chanukas habayis* (a dedication ceremony upon entry
to a new house or building). We came in from the extremely bitter cold
into an uncomfortable, stuffy, small house.

Once inside, we felt in our element, ignoring the heat and eager to
be parents to our spiritual children. The family shared with us and the
community the gift of celebration in their new house.

As *shluchim,* we juggle many roles and come to many events to bring
warmth and share the experience with our community. Perhaps, today
I will be a parent, friend, chef, or hostess. I was in luck, and I stepped
into the chef's shoes where we were directed to plate, taste, and design.

We were around a small kitchen counter, but it smelled of the perfume
of the many countries all our ancestors had lived in. This teeny home
also held a Sephardic feel and ambiance of Morocco, Yemen, Israel, and
Tunisia, with a small hint of South Africa thrown into the mix.

All of the children ran out of patience in the overly hot room. Their
high shrills caused the old, worn-out chandelier to vibrate. We stopped
our sentimental musings, and being emotional *Yiddishe* (Jewish)
mamas, a simple hysteria took hold of each one of us.

The shrills and screeching voices came from the little "unnoticeables"
in the large talkative crowd. These unnoticeables became noticed,
and their teeny, hungry little tummies then became our focus. I, with

hurried steps, organized the little kids' table. Plates, forks, cups, food, and water channeled calm to the children in the tiny room.

I heard loud footsteps coming from the crowd, and a heavy bent figure with a golden cane emerged from the mountains of people. His presence there was unexpected, and I stared down at a familiar face. Sometimes a familiar face is one we anticipate greeting, and sometimes we might try to avoid a face-to-face encounter.

As a *rebbetzin*, I always need to say hello to everyone and find out how each person is doing, but I couldn't find it in myself to do it this time. There was this cold awkwardness between us, and our hello was brief, with a simple nod, and we continued on our path of hellos amongst the crowd.

Luckily, a loud ring buzzed my sleepy phone. I was able to step outside the small, hot room and sit in my car. As I finished the call, my thoughts raced back to unfinished and forgotten business inside. The situation was hard for me to digest and difficult to embrace. I felt like I was at war to reclaim the crown in my own kitchen.

It seems like this took place so long ago. It was then a time of peace and excitement as we went through our daily routine. Each day had its own focus and guidelines that had to be met. The kitchen was where I was to be found. It was like soft music: preparing programs, Shabbos, and the little but important things. Even at the last moment's notice cooking still feels like music, but with a quicker beat to its rhyme.

He was then middle-aged and came to us with the desire to help. When one offers a hand, it is thankfully accepted, for who would dare to say no, especially after a few months of seeking a helper who was willing to be those extra hands which were so badly needed in a busy kitchen.

Shabbosim (many Shabbos) came and went, and this feeling crept up on me that this older gentleman had some ulterior hidden motive. At first, I gave him the benefit of the doubt. For who would come to a *rebbetzin's* kitchen if not to help?

Perhaps he was playing with the idea of expressing himself with food or with a special dish of his own that he wanted to show off. So, we worked together to make his famous breaded salmon and spicy salads.

One day, one of our Shabbos regulars came up to me with a little droplet of food and shyly asked for more. I had a recognition that my hard-earned *heimishe* atmosphere was silently fading away. I always made sure to make everyone feel at home, so that they felt comfortable going back for seconds.

Perhaps it was during this second moment of disappointment that a strange breeze crept up the back of my neck. I had a feeling of uneasiness about this older gentleman.

I shrugged it off and quickly served the rest of the fish. I began to pay closer attention to this gentleman's routine and noticed he would serve really small portions of food to the starving crowd. I quickly and gently whispered to him that we had plenty of fish, and that he could serve more to each person. He flat out refused with excuses. I didn't want to cause a problem, making "issues out of tissues," so I ignored what later became important signs.

As time passed, I began to feel like an outsider in my own kitchen. If I opened the door, he slammed it shut. When I arranged something some way, he rearranged it his own way. He always took credit for all of my hard work and claimed it as his own.

I am a quiet chef and one who abhors confrontation. However, sometimes you need to stand up before the kitchen roof comes crashing down around you.

I started to take control of my kitchen one step at a time. Soon enough, it became natural for me to be crowned as my own kitchen boss. I was glad and felt free to take the reins once again. I was still *heimishe* and kind, but now the boss of my own kitchen again.

As I sat in the car, my mind played out this little once-important story. I smiled, knowing that chapter was closed, and now everyone felt comfortable. I quietly opened the door to the house and was greeted by my little boys and a room full of many happy people.

It's a lesson for the soft-spoken person that prefers to step down rather than face the music. My message to them is that the confrontation doesn't need to be mean. It can be done in a nice and caring way. One just needs to firmly put the other in his place without backing down. Otherwise, it becomes a circle of mess all around you.

Some people have a misconception of what true leadership is. They feel a louder voice is the ultimate leader. The truth is that being a dedicated person who cares and wants to help their community is what it's all about.

the friendship of two little toddlers

Friendship can come from even the littlest among us.

i heard the pitter-patter of feet scurrying across the freshly washed floors. My apron wrapped tightly around me, I finished the last load of dishes and turned off the stove. There was a loud knock at the door: the children were here!

The sounds of excited shrieks coming from my little kids made them so happy about *gan* (little children's program), and they waited eagerly for the sound of the doorbell.

Three hectic, hectic, hectic weeks played a tug of war with my emotions. Should I keep the *gan* running throughout the week, or should I place it on the back burner for later?

I had mixed feelings. To begin with, I couldn't stuff more time into an hourglass that was filled to the brim. Each minute was counted for, and no one was coming to loan me more time.

It felt like there was a tremendous difficulty involved in making this special program part of our lives. Already, each moment was reserved for our *shlichus*. It appeared that there were no more hours left in the day to be planned. From the after-school program to the Friday night meal and each little treasured moment of giving, it was like the day was folding its arms and demanding that a good bookkeeper be held accountable.

Then the humor, love, and faith fell into my lap, and every day became a special occasion of sorts. I felt like my kids were waiting eagerly for the doorbell, with both my nose and theirs pressed against the glass in anticipation of the *gan* kids' arrival. The days were manipulated to fit these precious hours, about which we had no regrets.

One day while I was teaching, all of a sudden, I saw a huge spider. My normal calm demeanor was transformed; I was greatly concerned, and I found myself hurriedly grabbing the children to take them upstairs. One sweet little boy grabbed his friend's hand, and in desperation, clung to it so tightly as to never let it go.

I quickly announced to this little boy that *morah* (teacher) was holding his friend, and that everything was OK, but no matter how convincing I was, the hand still clung tightly to his little friend, even when the boy had no more strength and could barely move up the next step.

This was the silliest of moments to me, and it became the humor that crushed the "fear of the spider." After a few seconds, our classroom was back to how it should be—a room filled with a happy teacher and even happier children.

The deep impressions that we make on little children are powerful and surreal but have an even more profound and lasting effect than the teacher can even hope to realize. The innocence and honesty that kids can teach the world are powerful. From the happiest of smiles to being content with the simplest things, to the hugs and affection one receives from their tiny little hands, these things do wonders for us all.

There is a saying, "The little *kinderlach* (children) will bring about the *Moshiach* (Messiah)." Children are pure, and they have no deep inner desire for anything else; they have no trickery, greed, or selfish motives that stick like glue. Instead, there is pure desire, with hugs, laughter, and more, and this is the story of our *gan*. The teacher is empowered to uphold the life lessons which are taught, shared, and treasured by her little students.

I continued to teach *gan*, and I became inspired each day anew. It happened as time quickened its pace that I became fascinated with this newfound approach of using the children's perspective as a looking glass for each lesson learned. I cherished the results from the closed doors and secret chambers of the child's mind.

On *shlichus*, it's tough when some families move away and new ones come into town. You have to hope that every moment you spent with a particular kid will hopefully leave him or her inspired and confident.

However, the empty seat leaves an impact not just in the classroom but on you, and the parents feel more empowered and ready to know their child better when they do.

Goodbyes are never easy, and newcomers, although always welcomed, are not yet connected. Once children at *gan* break through their first real special moment, the friendship, connection, and journey can begin.

the man who needed a divorce

Sometimes, just giving a little can help out
much more than you would think.

it was a perfect Friday night, full of smiles and warm laughter which
could be felt and heard from the large room. The late hour was creeping
up on us, and one by one, my little children became like fallen soldiers,
slowly sliding off their chairs, soon to be sound asleep on the floor.

The last straw for me came when my husband forcibly tried to make
sure his eyelids wouldn't close completely shut. It was my signal to take
over the duties as the crossing guard, and I gently moved the fallen
soldiers one by one from the room.

"Rabbi, you must take the kids home, and the older ones will stay with
me to help me clean up," I suggested. It was like magic, and all my little
fallen soldiers became energized and awake, including the Rabbi.

"Mommy, it's time to go? Are you coming too?" I could see the pleas in
their little eyes, wanting me to tuck them all into their beds.

"No, boys. Mommy needs to clean up, and Tatty will put all of you to
bed," I said more gently, feeling their discomfort but knowing they were
in the best hands.

I had just started cleaning up from the Friday night meal when one of
the men staying over came to help me. I began to look for the hummus,
and it looked a bit different to me.

"Did you notice what happened to the hummus?" I said, trying to look
like everything was normal and not trying to alarm my guest.

"Oh, yes. I took it out of the garbage because the bag was clean. Here, look for yourself." He was excited and unbashful of his extra help, or so he thought.

All I could do was try to put on a false smile when an idea popped into my head. "Can you do me a favor and make sure that the last few things come downstairs to the kitchen?" I said, trying not to show my nerves at this hour.

"Sure, Rabbanit," he replied as he quickly went upstairs. As soon as his footsteps faded, I took the hummus and threw it out, knowing that we don't play by these rules in my kitchen.

Once he came back down, he began to tell me his life story. He looked like a person who had a tough life; it was late, so I was only half-listening but was being polite and not interrupting.

Finally, all the food was put away, and I walked upstairs to the Rabbi's office just to sit and rest my tired feet. When he knocked and wanted to continue to talk about his situation, I understood that even though my husband was helping him, he wanted to hear my perspective, my approach, and to know from a *rebbetzin's* viewpoint what he should do.

I was so exhausted from such a long week that I looked at him and thought, "Really, at this hour?" My expression must have said that, because he left the room and half apologized for the hour. I forced myself to get up even though I had tired limbs and was uncomfortable, and I readied myself for a long conversation because a congregant needed me.

I followed him to the meal table where my older kids in the corner were still playing chess and waiting for me to take them home. I let him speak and listened to his sad tale of what his marriage had become.

He explained to me that since the beginning, he felt that he was mismatched. Even when they were still newlyweds, his wife was abusive and started legal battles with lawyers. This dance of revenge perpetrated itself almost right away.

There were no breaks in the ups and downs of their disagreements, and many times he was permanently stuck in the dog house. This made it especially hard for him because he was a non-confrontational person and abhorred airing his dirty laundry in public.

Now it was eighteen years later, and this once strong man was utterly broken, full of sorrow over his own choices and decision making, or so he blamed himself. His children—all of them—called him only to embarrass and make fun of him. He gently asked them to stop interfering and calling him names, but they refused.

I, who hates confrontations, and I, who believes that there is a happy ending to every story, understood that I had to go against my very nature to help this fellow *Yid* (Jew) in need.

"How can I help you?" I heard myself exclaim, a bit too excited I noticed, which was very odd for me, especially when it came to this topic of divorce.

"Well, what do you think that I should do? Should I divorce my wife? She already has a restraining order against me! Won't it just get worse?" he said, with his face in his hands.

I yanked my normal non-confrontational reaction, stuck her in my pocket, and pulled out my motherly, no-nonsense approach. This was definitely a grown man in front of me who needed my help. I knew that if I didn't help him, he would crawl back into his corner and never come out again.

I looked to see if my kids could hear us, and they seemed very engrossed in their game to the point where maybe only an earthquake might make them look up. I needed to get a clearer picture. Divorce is a serious matter, and I felt I really needed to make sure that the situation is like he claimed it was, and not just a fight that the couple was having.

"Does your wife go to the *mikvah* (bath for spiritual purity)?" If they are at least intimate with each other, I could argue that she still loves him and should continue counseling. There was silence, and I began to feel that perhaps it was too personal a question, and there would be no hope for movement for him in his married life.

"No, we have not been intimate for over two years. I tried many times to work on the relationship, but she just makes fun of me, so I wait and hope maybe someday. But as of now, I know that she wants a divorce too," he said, now beginning to get more comfortable in his chair.

"OK. If that is the case, you need to get a lawyer and not be afraid to go to court and win. Do you have evidence that she beat you and hurt you?"

"Yes! I have all of it and plenty of documentation to prove my point," he said, a little impressed with himself, and he seemed to look like he could actually do this.

I knew it would be very hard for him, so I encouraged him to follow up with my husband. It seemed to work with the constant back-and-forth phone calls. My husband needed to be there for him like a long-lost brother who he felt at home with.

Finally, after a bitter, horrid, and long eighteen years, the marriage was coming to an end. In his marriage, he had nowhere to go, but was only abused and kept quiet about it. He was now free and ready to try to live his life without being afraid of his own shadow anymore.

Two weeks later, he told my husband and me that he could fight her in court with a lawyer on her false claim of abuse and win. He was beaming and so proud to finally be standing up for himself. He was ready to handle this, challenge it, and move on for real without as much baggage as he and we once thought.

He will overcome this and move onto the next step in a freer life, and when he is ready, he will find a worthy person to marry. He will no longer be afraid but will grow in confidence to be a better father and stand up to his children's verbal abuse with wit and patience.

the magic between two strangers

The bond is so strong between friends speaking in a foreign language, a language of old that only belongs to Jewish brethren.

the Shabbos flames flicker brightly, and the table begins to serve its guests. Their eyes are glued to one another as they catch up on old times. The table seems to hold time still, even when it's packed with the hurried beats of people in a Shabbos day rhythm.

The rabbi is always there for each person's needs. There is always time to talk to him and make sure you are noticed. This brotherly love between these friends seemed more of an unknown background. Perhaps the two have met before and are good friends. How else can one really explain this excitement and magic between two strangers?

There is a slaughterhouse close to our Chabad house, which means that many Israeli families come to work and live in the middle of a small but close-knit American Jewish community.

Our central community is made up of warm and *heimish* locals, and we embrace every person who knocks on our door. It's a community of the children of Avraham, Yitzchak, and Yaakov that now stands forlorn in its observance. Each person that we bump into is special no matter where they are from and who they are now. I always try to bring this mindset with me to be a *Yiddishe* mama to my congregation.

Many locals that we bump into are just dipping their toes in the waters of observance, but these Israeli families have been introduced at birth. Israeli families have the advantage of being born observant, but the disadvantage of everything else in our local area. The sweltering summers and the bitterly cold winters are definitely hard on a working American Jewish family, and they are that much harder on a foreigner.

As *shluchim,* we stand with them to make sure their spiritual and monetary needs are met. Sometimes, we have the community donate clothes, food, furniture, and temporary living quarters to make it possible.

Time creeps along, and weeks, months, and years pass on by. Like an outcast, after many years they still feel so alone. The language is difficult to master; the people surrounding them react kindly but remain an acquaintance at heart.

Only a few friends dare to take the plunge and take their fellow's hand to enter their own world of business. My husband and I work around the clock to make each lonely person feel happier and more comfortable, but this place does not always feel like home for them.

There was a new family that had arrived fresh from Israel. They soon found out that twins were on the way, and they were ecstatic, starting with double the joy. As time went on, the joy, though, seemed to have diminished, for they began doubting whether they should stay regardless of the price. They would reminisce with us about the life in Israel which they left behind: a place with family, life, and growth, and where everything seemed easier.

In a foreign country, reality started setting in for them concerning what had to be done now, and emotions would have to come and find their place later. This couple felt trapped in a box.

It was their own box of worry, which was being complicated by decisions, places, and hardships that had to be dealt with on their own. There they sat, staring at unfamiliar faces, packed in the waiting room to see the doctor.

A phone call was made, and the rabbi, my husband, was on the way. Busy he is: the work of an emissary doesn't allow for even a second's break. The caring, understanding, and painful awareness that the rabbi, too, was once a foreigner drives him to come help each person in need.

It seemed like each week another Israeli couple was in dire need of our help. Someone was sitting in the waiting room, sad, alone, and without a word of understanding between her and the staff. Sure enough, a call was made, and my husband went to help this family, that family, and another in need. No heart was to break or sadness to be reeled in under his watch.

Meanwhile, time was ticking by, and the family expecting twins were told that their bundles of joy would arrive soon. The couple became very worried and wanted a Hebrew translator for each decision that the staff would make. It was late at night but determined not to leave a Jew in need, the rabbi came to join this family once again.

After a long back-and-forth translation and the late hour stood closer in the doorway, it was this last buzzer that hinted it was time to go home. The rabbi then said his goodbyes and left a room filled with happy faces.

A doctor watched him closely and saw that his heart was full of truth, that this rabbi truly enjoyed helping others. The doctor, with courage, approached him and said that he, too, was Jewish.

The doctor then excitedly continued and said that he was watching this rabbi from afar for many months and was inspired by how many people he helped for nothing else but the smile and happiness that spread across their faces.

The twins came home, and we came with many others to make this special day count for them. Laughing, singing, *l'chaim* (to life) was said, and it was almost forgotten that they were not in Israel, the Holy Land. Their faces glowed with joy, and they felt less lonely on that special day.

So, just like that, a family was truly inspired and affected by a hero of kindness. This family with twins was eternally grateful and forever stamped with this rabbi's kind touch. The couple kept in close contact with us even when they went back to Israel.

My husband and his friend have continued maintaining their strong friendship for close to ten years. The special bond was formed between these two strangers who became like brothers—like Yonasan and David, there was no friendship and love like theirs. What should have been a rivalry for the throne, almost by accident, turned and grew into the most talked of friendship and examples of loyalty in the Torah.

Time, distance, *Sephardic* versus *Ashkenazic* (different Jewish traditions)—no barrier could stop this friendship from blossoming. When a Jewish heart is touched, it ignites the soul's urge to touch back in a real, Jewish, and Divine way.

there's no competing with a legend

It can happen that regardless of one's efforts,
some things are just not meant to be.

there was a team of men, master garbage collectors, who suddenly came to an old building. It was a spiritual dwelling with a sliver of mystery that had rooms spilling over with many memories and experiences of people from different backgrounds.

Highly experienced, these collectors were just coming to do their job, oblivious to the Jewish center's history. They came to collect what they thought was unusable. The people there had this common thread that seemed to lace together even the most different of human beings. They were united by a very special old woman and her husband. A woman from the old country drew those into her corner of protection, and she did so with gentleness and love.

Years and years of dedication to her people left her imprint on them, and they became her children. Some tried to pull away but couldn't because the family's connection with her kept them close. After fifty years of raising, cherishing, and upholding her gathered people, a new couple came to take over.

It became obvious that only a hairbreadth of time had passed: the position of *shlichus* that we dreamt would go so smoothly was trapped in iron chains and wouldn't budge. Our energy and youth pleading to have an impact fell helplessly to the floor. We weren't here to compete, for it was her invitation and call to us that brought us here. But that didn't matter, for we were unwelcome—no matter how much effort we put in to try and succeed.

"Wow, they're here!" I said excitedly.

"Already?" the rabbi, my husband, said after wiping his brow after a long day of clearing and cleaning up old things.

These were furnishings that didn't belong in a beautiful Jewish center, or so we thought. There were broken chairs, odd-looking dressers, and even some old rags. It felt great cleaning out the clutter, rearranging books, and tweaking the old tune and rhythm to a faster beat.

We were here to take over a beautiful Jewish community and felt a clean, new beginning was the right step moving forward. It didn't cross our minds that sometimes new and modern isn't always the right approach for a very established place.

It was a promise that we had hoped would be kept and embraced, but it was not in our cards. All sides were collapsing in on us. This legend of a woman sadly didn't see eye-to-eye with our style and approach.

The modernistic feel that we gave to spruce up the rooms looked out of place in this building which seemed to come from another time. The rooms' era was that of our great-grandparents, and it made them feel weighted and cheap, like a burden that felt so out of touch with the regular, mismatched style of old.

As we tried to be the grandmaster fixers and organizers, it became crystal clear that we were not far behind what the garbage collectors had taken. The group felt too closed to let us slip inside it, and no matter how much we pushed the circle, it would not budge open.

We didn't want to fail a beautiful community and their legend, so we pushed even harder and felt a deep thirst to prove ourselves. We tried becoming more innovative and creative, but the circle kept pushing us out. Unlike most communities, the people refused to mold themselves to us, their rabbi and *rebbetzin*.

We were determined to find acceptance. We graciously bought these beautiful, decorated dividers as our customary *mechitzah* (room dividers); I thought that they would look great and bring a more elegant but modern feel to the division of seating between men and women. The room dividers were held to the letter of the law but had that added touch of elegance and modernity that took a person inside the modern era.

A few weeks passed, and I thought that maybe we won, and people liked the new look. Then a young woman just over six feet tall began bobbing her head over just to catch my shocked reaction. The whispers that followed made me think that perhaps I should bring out the long, flowing, dated curtain instead.

It then happened that we were invited to the community *havdalah*, a formal prayer marking the end of Shabbos. It portrayed light, promise, hope, and peace, but it didn't help us find our place in this tight group. I looked around and saw mixed emotions, more enhanced than usual, and wondered, what secret am I missing?

Is there writing on the wall that I glanced over? No, it must be just my nerves and my overzealous worry about fitting in. However, as the spices were being passed around and the candle stood high in tradition, I knew the end of our leadership was near.

After barely a year of *shlichus,* a position and place where emissaries live, it was over, and sadly enough, we tasted the bitterness too. The door slammed shut. As the cars pulled away and the crowd grew smaller and smaller, I knew that it would be the last time that we would stand in the Chabad house's doorway.

the priest, the rebbetzin, and the jew

G-d is found in every difficulty and success we have in life.

a helicopter took him above the night's dark sky, and he was air-lifted to the hospital, where decisions would be made which would determine if he would live or die.

Would G-d claim such an innocent young man? Would a family lose their father forever? So good a man but not of our faith! His Jewish wife was sad and heartbroken for her loss.

A young Jewish woman yearns to be comforted by an emissary, begging to be told that everything and everyone will be ok. A shul is the place where she demanded to be, and yet she never cared about her faith before, until this terrible catastrophe happened.

Instead, she was running from it and hiding from her heritage, afraid of how to deal with her Judaism and wondering, what would that mean in one's life?

Far away from her people and the shul was her life. Happy was her existence with two children and a secular lifestyle. When she was reminded of who she was and where she was going, it changed her outlook. A tragic accident shook up her life, and now she was at a loss and didn't know where she belonged.

Her aunt kept messaging me that her niece was living with a *goy* (a non-Jew) in the middle of nowhere, that her husband was in a bad accident, and that her niece wanted to pray to *Hashem* (G-d). Yet, I was told that I shouldn't push her niece about her Judaism or to become more religious, because this was off-limits.

I understood the aunt was overprotective, but it was laughable how little she knew about Chabad. She clearly must have been confusing us with someone else. Chabad is all about giving to others and showing them how to take things at their own pace and time.

Yet, what really mattered was helping this Jewish woman in her earth-shattering, devastating new reality. I quickly replied, "Yes, and when can we meet?"

Shortly after we spoke, I decided to cancel all of my plans for the day with a new hope of helping a young mother in her time of need and pain.

I found myself hurrying up to the Chabad house with giant raindrops coloring the sidewalk with emotion. It was a rainy day, and a car pulled up with a young mom, tears flowing freely down her face.

She carefully walked up the ramp, and I quickly, without hesitation, embraced her and held her for a long moment. It allowed her to cry and feel she was not alone in her pain, even though we were strangers. Rained on and cold, we entered the Chabad house and slowly let the shul warm us up both spiritually and physically.

I offered tea and coffee, and we finally sat down with a prayer book. She looked at the pages as if studying them intently and then looked up with a confused face. "What is it?" I asked curiously.

She said to me, "I don't remember how to read from the prayer book, but it's a relief to be looking at the book that tells me who I am."

I stared at her, thinking about what she was saying. So, I said gently, "Care to explain to me?"

"Oh, well, it was terrible. My husband is in an induced coma, and I don't even want to think about what will happen to him. He was helping a friend move a refrigerator, and it fell on him.

"Why does he always want to help people? I don't know! Just look, he probably will die, and all for what, helping his friend?"

She took a deep breath and started crying but stopped herself and continued, "His family came to grieve over their son and be with me, but they brought their priest as well. They are trying to make me convert. I'm not sure I can go back because I feel so worried that they will succeed, and I know it's not who I am."

"Really?" I was too shocked to say anything else. I know it happens, but so openly? In this country? At this horrific time in their lives? This caught me by surprise!

This Jewish girl who had been living a secular life was still passionately fighting to keep her Judaism. Her bravery nearly knocked me off my already wobbly chair.

I tried to allow her to calm down. I decided to drink some tea to calm myself down a bit as well. We then together looked at her prayer-book pages.

She then continued, "I don't want to be observant, but I don't want to be non-Jewish either. I'm a Jew, and I don't really know what that is, but I know that is who I am."

I stared at her and couldn't believe her honesty and her desire to be closer to Hashem, even though she did not know what that meant. I told her that whatever she needs, I'm here for her, and she can go at her own pace. She thanked me, and we started davening *Minchah* (the afternoon prayer).

Afterward, we sat down again, and she wanted to know more. "What can I do because I feel so helpless. It's the waiting to know if he'll be alright that's killing me," she half muttered, looking nervously at me.

I thought about asking her to write a *pan* (a letter to the Rebbe), but knew she was not into writing. She had never written a letter to place at the Kotel (the Western Wall) or to anyone holy, let alone to the Rebbe.

So I said to her, "Perhaps, you can write a letter to your husband for when he wakes up about how you feel about him and your children."

"You're right! I would love to write to him, but I'm not sure what to say," she said, hesitating, but her eyes finally lit up.

"Oh, I'm sure you will think of something. And you can take the notebook and the prayer books with you to the hospital if that will help you feel better about all of this," I said, trying to be reassuring, but not too firm. I wanted her to be happy with her decisions and feel comforted in her time of pain.

"Ok," she said, and she left.

The next day, she called me and told me she felt more in control with her prayer book. She also read her husband the letter that she wrote, and he woke up and was able to speak a little bit to her.

"Wow, that's awesome! Can I bring you some homemade kosher food?" I offered excitedly, hoping she would take me up on my request.

"No! My mother-in-law brought me her homemade food already, so I'm good."

Oy, I thought to myself, her first action after all of this is to have non-kosher food. It is the same person, her mother-in-law, who tried to convert her with the priest, but I heard myself say, "Well, have a good night, and if you change your mind, then let me know."

Her husband ended up recovering and is working slowly towards a full recovery. I was so happy for her on the one hand, but on the other, I felt she was leaving behind the experience of knowing what her Jewishness is all about.

When people recover and things are going well, does that mean that it's over for one's relationship with G-d?

I still have hope, and my *Shabbat Shalom*'s are sent weekly. Sometimes they are ignored, and sometimes they are responded to. Regardless of whether she responds or not, I want to still be in touch with her.

The Rebbe made sure that all of his *shluchim* go out and hold the hands of each person: diamonds in our community. The members of the community then become our children—our sons and daughters who we struggle to raise, but at the end of the day, it's up to each child or person to choose what's right and choose life!

lonely sailors

A sailor is one who sails the seas and tires himself in the storm as he hopes and waits to settle down on the shore.

the sailors are lonely people that dare not settle down. The internal desire for a companion on their journeys is a need that they rarely feel. They get used to being rejected and understand that this is the price they have to pay for rarely standing still.

Each holiday, program, Friday night, or birthday party, a fun-loving and old uncle comes to celebrate with us. He is the one who is always holding my boys on his lap or patting them on the back when they feel sad.

Surprisingly, he never looks tired and is regularly volunteering to help one way or another. Even though his work is his badge of honor, he never gets more than a few hours of sleep each night.

This older uncle is now almost sixty-eight, and each time he comes to visit, he mentions how he wishes he had gotten married. If only he had grabbed the opportunity to meet someone and settle down...

He recently began to look sad, which is never a garment that he comfortably wears. Unfortunately, it was way too late when he started reminiscing about taking the giant leap, and like a loyal servant, bitterness clung tightly to this regretful, kind uncle.

He was ready to retire, and after a lifetime of living his life—which was his work—he came home to no one and had nobody to share his vacations and experiences. He was all alone, and it is that much more challenging as he gets closer to his retirement.

The constant reminder that plagues him was that he would be only called uncle and would just be a visitor; he has only the dream of a constant companion, but not the real thing.

A friend, confidante, or companion is a dream only for those of privilege, or so the sailor feels. It's a privilege to have not just needs fulfilled but also desires and dreams. The effort for this type of task is tough, especially when it's placed in a sailor's hectic work-filled weeks.

It begins very innocently for these lonely sailors: a few more years of college, maybe grad school, or embrace the company at work and save up extra money. The years start flying by, and one wakes up no longer twenty-three but thirty-three. It then becomes much harder to imagine oneself as a married person.

He, the traveling sailor, enjoys and celebrates his own decision-making in life. The non-changes and non-compromises on his path of strict comfort feel like the calm sea before the storm. The sailor, unwilling to leap over the fence, becomes frozen with lost time. He then fears that working towards a solution and letting another inside will be scary and bleak.

The idea of *serious* sacrifices—working as two and not one—is much harder on the one who hesitates to roll up his sleeves and go outside his own comfort zone. He feels so far away from settling down, and for an older lady or gentleman, it becomes virtually impossible.

We have all kinds of people entering our Chabad house doors, each with his or her own story of what keeps him or her from taking the next step in life: marriage. The step from boyhood to manhood or the step from girlhood to womanhood holds them back; for most, it becomes the mission and journey each day to seek out where one's soul mate is hiding.

However, there are a select few who can't or perhaps who are frightened to turn the corner. Sometimes we can gently push them along the path to marriage, and sometimes they are not ready and never truly choose to be ready.

A great chef came to town from South America. He was absolutely brilliant with each creation he placed in front of us. One was more beautiful than the next, and sure enough, five new entrees made their way to greet us.

After a while, I was thankful for his cooking and got to know him as a person. He was going through a messy divorce, and it had a big impact on him. He soon became a regular sailor, not wanting to move on or find a new partner in life. His priorities and determination were not those of true responsibility, and nothing could make him change his focus.

No matter how sad, lonely, or empty his days may have felt, this sailor didn't want to put in any effort. We chose to just watch from the sidelines. This was his way and his mindset; he was not willing to be bereft of any physical need that he might ultimately want.

I felt bad for this sailor: In truth, how could it be his fault? He was dealt a rotten hand with a first marriage that crushed him on all levels as a person. The parents, grandparents, and dear friends of this sailor were frustrated with his life's decisions and eventual turnout. He was still in his thirties, utterly devastated and still young; making this sailor's story that much sadder.

Each sailor hopes he can settle down and find true happiness with a wife, children, and a house to host guests. It becomes complicated and more difficult to make this a reality, especially if one went through a rough marriage to begin with, and therefore a second one can seem pointless.

The sailor needs to stop rehashing his past and not give in to the fears of not having enough to give his partner, whether it is a physical, emotional, or mental form of giving. Perhaps it's the silliness of the human race not wanting to get into the constant uncomfortable drama that can happen as a father to his children or perhaps a mother to hers.

It could even be more bothersome: the pressure of what may lay ahead as a husband to his wife, or a wife to her husband, especially if one witnessed one's parents' or friends' messy divorce.

The South American chef's story truly touched my soul, and I had to try to help out this sailor, so I let my mind turn its matchmaking wheels. Soon, I remembered that I had a friend in New York who was still not married. She, too, was a sailor and got comfortable controlling each step that needed to be taken, which meant that an unpredictable marriage had no place in her heart.

It is hard for one to go and try to help out the sailors. The few times that I had the nerve to sit them down and ask them where life had landed them or encourage them to change their focus, the response was always negative or unknown, and never a real desire to change.

I remember that I once bumped into the wrong sailor, and he screamed and yelled at me until the whole *shul* cleared itself out, and everyone pretended to be admiring the outdoors. *Baruch Hashem* (Blessed is G-d) it was a beautiful sunny day, and our close community had the decency not to get involved.

It went from a hushed, gentle, private conversation to a response that I would never forget. It didn't change my way or passion for trying to help others. I realized that I had to experience this tornado-like moment for whatever reason, and I felt a deep sadness for this troubled sailor, for there clearly was a strong emotional pain harboring itself on his shores.

One can argue that a career or set job is better than being stuck with a family life, where effort has to be put in, and not always does one reap the rewards. Things can fall apart, and many losses can happen—feelings that keep the belief in fate close and Divine Providence at arm's length.

Even if it can be tough and you can even empathize with the traveler, a step towards the next journey in life is very much needed. Perhaps, as a kid, the sailor was not yet ready to graduate from high school. He became the one unmotivated to dive in and preferred being comfortable for a short while, which was better than the decision to get married.

I wanted to bring these sailors true happiness, so I spoke to them, and the sailor chef agreed, but my older friend did not. She wasn't ready to dive into a new way of life and preferred her comfortable space and place. It would be challenging and mean starting a new life that would change all of her comforts and allow another inside her domain, fortress, and inner decision-making.

The divorced sailor was sad about being rejected but understood it was not to be taken personally. However, it had a deep impact on him and motivated this sailor to really reflect on his life. The *rebbetzin* believed in him, and people believed that he deserved a second chance at happiness; he wasn't doomed to sit out the rest of his life and watch others have the dream that he truly deserved.

It seemed that this was the last push for the chef sailor to become serious about choosing to get uncomfortable in order to become truly happy. So, it turned out that a few months later, the sailor got engaged and found such happiness that others wished that they could slide into his shoes.

On the other hand, my friend is still single and comfortable in her sailor world. Will she ever care to step out of the comfortable fortress that life has set her up with and dare to venture out into the unknown?

Perhaps, time and patience will tell her story. To find happiness, one must embrace the fact that life will be chaotic and not perfectly controlled. That is the only way to really jump on the bandwagon of life.

hope inside the corner

Hope is really embracing Divine intervention.

there are dancing circles of hope and excitement in every little girl who matures into a young woman. It is she who demands the same love and support as in her youth. It becomes her fear of perchance not having the privilege to hold, love, and cherish a child of her own. This passion burns deep within her but just as much does the tagalong of worry poke at her nerves each day.

The curious young girl then blossoms into the woman, the mother, and the dream; finally, her wish and hope has come true. It was her tenacity and perseverance which brought about the fruition which was finally hers.

It was a Hebrew school morning, and then came the race of who would come and who wouldn't come in "The Frozen Tundra" of our city. The cars glistened white; the snow was on everything, cold and frozen, which succeeded in making the sidewalks bare of people.

As it is with all emissaries, we try to push hard for parents to come and overcome the difficulties. Forty years ago, they, the parents, used to plead with the shuls, the synagogues of old, for a spot to place their child amongst his or her peers.

It was more understood in previous generations that Jewish learning mattered, and deep sacrifices were simply a part of bringing one's child to a better tomorrow.

Unfortunately, today's parents' worries are less noble in faith. The push for a Jewish child to succeed sometimes needs to come from the rabbi and the *rebbetzin* themselves. They are a couple loaned to a community, and it is their job to help each little or big person succeed.

I always wondered how to describe what a Chabad house is like to the many people who knock on our door. A Chabad house: It is perhaps your new neighbor on the block that moves in and seems always to offer something to you and your family, whether you were in the mood for a gift or not. At Chabad, the neighborhood adjusts to the friendly intrusions and looks forward to the next pleasant encounter.

It would often happen that no matter how I would promise to make a child's adjustment easier, some families wouldn't budge, and surprisingly, this was true for even the more observant ones.

I was confused at this mistake, and at some point decided that I didn't really want to know this answer of theirs, or did I? What held them back?

It was too late and too honest; comments, comments, and more comments flowed freely from a usually reticent, tight-lipped woman. My push and warmth to bring the families closer had helped me discover the truth.

The Hebrew school families had plenty of boys, but no girls her daughter's age. To make matters worse, her niece was still unsure if she was ready to come. This left her daughter the only single Jewish girl in her class, and she wasn't interested in putting her daughter through it all, even if that meant no Jewish school.

"If only, Rabbanit ["rabbi's wife" for Israeli Jews], you had a daughter my little girl's age, I could send her," she said quietly. My throat felt like a frog was in it, and my usual friendly self felt bereft of words and even though it was odd, I started to relax with the very thick silence surrounding us.

There was nothing to say. How could I explain to this Jewish woman that it hurt me to be reminded of it? When it came to girls, it was as if I was childless. I have never felt that sense of motherhood to a little girl, and the feeling of passing down the line to the next generation of Jewish women. That sense of relief and comfort has never sat on my porch.

After this incident, the occasions kept overlapping each other, almost as if fate kept giving me these reminders, but nothing could be done, and there was no one to blame. Children were gifts and blessings: the sons and the daughters.

What would happen if, by chance, there would be no succession, no passing down to another? How many times do we wonder about this fate? What will be, who will protect what we have stood for, stood against, and dreamt about?

Since the minute of the candles circling the groom and breaking the glass, the countdown begins in the world of matrimony. Who, what, when, and how soon can the new generation begin?

Some have careers, and for many, this is a career! The job of raising and uplifting the newcomers, the little children, in our old ways of life.

At many events at our Chabad house, plenty of young mothers come, and I pass strollers full of cute ruffles with bows and ribbons. Silly little laughs fill the already noisy room; these mothers find comfort with their daughters and can be heard shushing the baby dolls to sleep.

In the beginning, I knew, at some point, my turn would come, because it is the way of the mind to think so. It's our right, and then one believes our wish, and our desire to have our needs met.

Sometimes, what's in our hearts does not always come to fruition. Like each year, I contributed to the newcomers of our future and continued my hectic role as a mother, and I began to do some introspection on my role as a proud mother of the boys only club. It became a club with seven of them, and it was a close club where each of them had fun, love, and plenty of hard-earned rewards and treats.

After thirteen years, it dawned on me that this is my dream, but is it the reality that is meant to be for me? What does G-d want of me? Perhaps the boys only club will keep climbing, and maybe this is the way it's supposed to be.

"What complaints can I have when the glass is half full, tipped for my eyes to see?" I wondered out loud. It is a peek, a rare glimpse, a dream, or even a desire to know what will be in the future of one's life. Perhaps the patience is lost in our group or club of those who yearn for a daughter.

If it is not meant to be, what right do we have to yearn, beg, and plead? G-d is the Healer, the Knower, and the final Judge. However, it is the way of mothers to push and to have what their hearts want. We want the chance to give a claim to the future club of Jewish mothers.

The mind, though, is a tricky fellow; he follows the heart of demands, wishes, and rights. Up and down the seesaw, the mind is in a vicious cycle of feeling sorry for itself. It will take only one little cold, piercing wind of negativity until the proudly lit candle flickers low and its embers die out.

As if on cue, an angel is sent to the door, and a distraction of sorts then uplifts you again. Perhaps, it is good news or someone in need who can lift your spirits for a while. The candle is one's soul, one's will to cling to G-d and stand strong with Him.

It's the way of life, the bitter battle of not always having the dream, and the fervent hope that we will succeed in what we desire. My place, one's place, and G-d's place are then turned over to Him inside one's corner of grief, even if it feels like the corner is closed to outsiders.

To the one who grieves, still held in her corner, I say that one should not forget to let G-d grieve with you and hold you in the time of your need. His glass is always full, and He always sees what's true and right, and He just might even gift wrap for you one of the biggest miracles of life: the next of kin.

The freedom from her worry of the burdens of life don't hold sway over her, in the urgency to do what's right. She hopes the wish she had in her younger years will be fulfilled for her older self. It will then pass on to the next generation—their humor, stories, and memories from an older generation.

the scent of an angel

Like the footsteps in the sand, it is then that G-d carried us.

whatever the holiday, I always find myself in a bit of a squeeze: lists being organized, things being laid out to cook with, and every inch of my kitchen cleaned. It's hectic, it's *meshuggah*, and it's *shlichus*.

Sometimes, I'm lucky, and I'll have a *malach* (angel) in whichever circumstance I find myself in. I find G-d is always walking beside me, making His imprint on the path of my life. Divine providence is the moment G-d lets you know He is there.

It was an enjoyable time that was full of life and lessons learned. I loved the brand-new Chabad house. There were even little tiny guest rooms for people that wanted to stay for Shabbos.

It was the holiday during the week where everything and everyone stood still. It was filled with that aura of peace and harmony that ever so gently makes room for each one of us again.

On *shlichus*, it's the hustle and bustle of preparations that eats at us—we want to make the impossible possible. It was my job as the rabbi's wife to make sure that everyone had what they wanted and needed at the time they arrived at our doorstep.

I was very grateful that people were very accommodating and helped out with the preparations for Shabbos and holidays in return. Sometimes, the ones who needed your help turned out to be the ultimate helpers.

It was Erev Pesach (right before Passover), and I came to a quiet kitchen, where nothing stirred except the humming of the refrigerator. I stared at the counters overburdened with raw vegetables piled up and overflowing. I tried to push away my anxiety that this year might be a lonelier and much more laborious time than usual.

My goal was to embrace the values of our heritage and make Pesach sing its song of remembrance. I began reminiscing about all my different helpers and *malachim* (angels) along the way. I thought it couldn't hurt and might motivate me to tackle this hours-long ordeal.

In one of my *mazel*-moments (a moment of good luck), a Moroccan man needed a place to stay. Purim was around the corner, and I would soon once again be a mother. To my surprise, he offered to help cook and serve everything. I couldn't have been more thrilled and relieved, as I was reminiscing about my positive, sweet memories and enjoying the thoughts of previous years. It turned out that a couple had just arrived from Israel in desperate need of a place to stay. So, of course, even with Passover being just a week away, the answer was, as always, "Yes, please stay."

The ifs and hows along the way would be figured out later. It seemed like I would have help after all. I felt myself glowing with excitement and smelled the sweet scent of Divine providence peeking in the doorway.

After the long rollercoaster ride at my own home, I finally headed towards the Chabad house for a long night's work. When I arrived, it was as if my eyes were seeing but not believing. In the twilight, the young couple was busy fulfilling their hard-earned title of expert potato peelers.

I was surprised at this hour to see the enthusiasm of my new angels. It was a bit embarrassing when I turned to them both and said, "It looks like I have some angels this year after all." They both laughed and continued to peel potatoes because what is Passover without potatoes?

It happened this same Passover that an unexpected incident left me speechless. I was walking to the Chabad house for the *Seder* (Passover meal) with my boys when in great haste, a large, apparently ownerless dog suddenly ran across the street.

The old joke about Jews and dogs seemed to play in my mind. However, the other part of my mind was figuring out how to protect my kids from a creature larger than they were. I carefully dared myself to stand between the stray dog and my boys.

Suddenly, a stranger jumped out of his car and took the dog by his collar. The timing was incredible; my boys could have been hurt and were saved by a *malach*.

I said, "Is this your dog?"

"No," he replied. "I'll take the dog to a shelter," he said. I thanked him and carefully walked around the seventy-five-pound dog.

On my way back, I realized angels come in all shapes and sizes. So it turns out that Hashem (G-d) never leaves us alone. We just have to open our eyes to the reality of Divine providence in our daily lives.

Sometimes, it's hard to have total and complete faith in G-d. Perhaps, we will step into a moment where we clearly see His canvas of life, where each moment is carefully planned. All the little steps in life are bursting with miracles coming out at the seams of the G-dly paintings of life.

We then try harder to believe in Him always, even with a dog the size of a horse approaching one's little defenseless treasures. Each one must take the "leap of faith" in Hashem, and He will then, in return, open the door of miracles for you.

the shivah house

When the fire dies, and the hailstorms are at rest again,
a new life can slowly comfort us over the old one.

the Rabbi and I pulled up to the funeral home. Our eyes sought
out a group of people we knew well. Each face was contorted with the
confusion that spread over the congregants like prey standing in plain
sight of its predator. Their limbs held the look of being motionless, and
their thoughts were far away in a cloud of grief.

It felt like we were trapped in this new world of hopelessness and
pain. As emissaries, we feel that pain has no chance to be embraced
and internalized for the here and now but is left on a shelf collecting
dust for later.

The mother, our friend, stood so alert, but her eyes looked dead and
weighted. The people, her guests, stood behind her like good supportive
friends, ready to be told that it's time to walk to the cemetery. We then
greet them as mourners, and we, as their emissaries, slowly escort them
to a place of forced silence.

It was a pretty day with fresh grass and blossoming flowers that were
ready to be smelled and picked. Our eyes, though, saw nothing but dark
gray cement. Our deep concentration became a balancing act with one
foot in front of the other.

The community, our spiritual children, entered the cemetery. They
helplessly froze, not really believing that this was the reality. Their feet
had taken them to a familiar courtyard of the deceased. One would
think that this would make one feel welcome, but our hearts and minds
held only grief.

My husband and I pulled ourselves out of our own trance and box of sorrow that we felt for our congregants and their tragic day of pain. We then found the strength to embrace the parents of the deceased. This wonderful mother, usually the life, energy, and hope of all situations and outcomes, stood there sobbing.

No hand on her shoulder or whispered kind words could stop the flow of her tears. Her little grandkids could hold back their rain of sorrow no longer and cried while holding her skirt tightly.

My husband, the Rabbi, in an emotionally filled voice, began the prayers for the burial. The community clenched their fists, tightly filled with dirt, and each took his turn pouring it on the open grave. We watched the dirt fly inside the freshly dug earth. It flew over the casket and buried what was once a daughter, a mother, and a friend.

The reaction of those who came was clear: shock, alarm, and most unsure of where to stand, act, or be. The chaos was obvious to the regular onlooker who passed by, but to bereaved hearts and our close-knit community, it all seemed right.

My husband started in a deep, mournful tune, and then, in unison, we pleaded with our Maker to be woken up from this nightmare.

As the last mounds of dirt were placed over the casket, the tortured reality hit, and horrid screams, like from a wounded animal, escaped my friend's lips. The rules of decorum could hold their reins no longer and were swept carelessly away. It allowed for painful emotions to surface and be free from their constraints.

They then allowed themselves to express their pain out loud. All of our eyes were wet from watching this mother lose her daughter right in front of us. This is a story that never should happen, but a mother buried her only daughter forever on this day.

When the funeral was over, we slowly, with lowered heads, walked back to the funeral home. It was like a ton of bricks were weighing down on our shoulders, and each step felt like hours and hours until our destination.

As we all finally arrived, we were careful in the performance of our laws and customs for a house of *shivah*, a period of seven days' formal mourning for the dead. We washed our hands in ritual and entered a beautiful house that was now saddened with *shivah*.

We sit silently with them as they sit on lowered stools, quiet but comforting. This rule of *shivah* is apparent: no talking unless spoken to by the family of mourners. The silence should not feel cold or aloof, but as a friend holding one upright in their time of pain. The rabbi and I sat close to them with a silence of respect, not daring to engage in conversation unless asked.

After a while, we walked around the house, and small little groups made their own chit chat of words with low tones and whispers. We finally found our places and watched the family mourn, and we were their voice when all that enveloped them was pain.

Two brothers started a row of petty arguments. One was tall, dark, and intellectual, while the other was large, blond, and emotional. Their quarrels seemed to come from a different time. Perhaps their sister's passing brought up old wounds, and her death dug out the flesh that had never healed.

The details, facts, and arguments were not meant for us, and we pretended the hurtful words and quarreling were not on display for all to see.

After some time had passed, the kind grieving man held both of his sons' hands. It was clear that this was a firm but silent means of comfort. This, in return, succeeded in quenching their thirst to thrash out, and the quarreling subsided. In its place, though, stood a vulnerable sadness.

It was a sadness that enveloped the room, and no moment felt darker than the one we sat inside. Finally, the intellectual boy sat down with his brother and decided to have a productive conversation. Their beautiful sister was dead, and the two kids that she left behind had a non-Jewish father. They wanted to figure out a way to keep both children in their home and their faith, but sadly, they knew that this was not meant to be.

The daughter was a teenager already and was able to choose to live with her Jewish grandmother. Being only six, the boy would have no choice but to go and live with his non-Jewish grandmother. She was a religious woman—a Roman catholic—and with him in her care, the obvious would happen to him. Their only hope to keep him Jewish and embrace their faith was to try to stay in touch with him. They clasped onto this hope that he would pass on the traditions of old.

So, just like that, cruelty took on many forms; it was a day of grieving for a mother who lost her daughter, children who lost their mother, and a sister and brother who lost each other forever.

After a while, we headed back home to another day, living the life of *shluchim*. Some days are happy, some are sad, and some are full of giving and grieving. The journey is to touch and affect each little light and help it to grow brighter and bigger. So, life goes on with one day down and a lifetime of dedication to go.

the silent partner

Like the footprints in the sand at the hardest of times,
it is then that He carries you and holds you upright.

a silent hero: he is a partner who patiently waits to carry it all on his shoulders. Whatever has fallen or been strewn aside, he picks up and walks beside to where you are going. This silent partner makes sure that you are never alone and never letting anyone down.

The programs are going great, and each day I'm in the rhythm of doing *peulah* (a program to help people) after *peulah*. It feels like the city is on fire with good deeds, and the noise and smiles confirm it. Then life slows down, and another baby is born. I sit there at a loss of what to do.

I force myself just to get up and deal with each little and big worry that falls in my lap. It sounds like everything is in control, in line, and perfect.

However, what happens when I'm pregnant, right after birth, or needed by the family? Who picks up the pieces to hold everything and everyone together with steady hands, so no one falls, including me?

Each day, I wake up and feel compelled to do more for the Rebbe, more for the community, and more for my children. The need to place everything on my shoulders is like a habit or second nature for me. How should I begin to get it all done once again?

Although my husband made special things for me on many occasions, this time, his help was most needed. His silence was most peaceful and kind, for he wouldn't even take credit for his hard work. I mentioned what great things he did, and he asked me quietly not to say a word about it.

It is the nature of a woman to need to be thanked, appreciated, and complemented at each little turn. Yet, he stands by me without a word or a need for compliments.

It was Erev Rosh Hashanah (right before the holiday), and my soul fought a battle with itself. I wanted to fly to get everything done and to be able to greet all of our guests: the Chabad family. But I knew after giving birth to my seventh son that I needed to rest.

The idea of rest in general for me is torture, especially when guests are eagerly coming through the doors, which are open with people flooding through the Chabad house chambers. This electricity whooshes through you, and it feels like bliss—an excitement that touches your limbs, and that negates any need or idea of rest.

Inside and outside, my door of worry kept swinging like it was confused somehow. The feeling of responsibility and the mother within wanted so much to do what I've always done, but I knew that to be the best mother, I would then have to rest and let others take hold of the reins.

The sweat on his brow and tiredness on my husband's face said it all. I pleaded with him to let me help do something to make his load a bit less weighted. His smile and need to make his wife, children, and community happy took away the fight to plead.

It was over and useless to argue, for the answer was already written this year in the Book of Life. As a new mother, I must rest and watch the family step into making everything alright. Sometimes, Hashem (G-d) will give you a silent partner even if you try to resist it.

I watched behind the *mechitza* (the room divider for the men and women) with worry and fear. After many sleepless nights with our new son, would my overburdened silent partner succeed with his general role as rabbi too? The prayers, singing, speaking, and standing for hours, would this wear and tear him down?

I watched him sing and pray in his usual deep, concentrated mode of prayer, and the *taleisim* (prayer shawls) filled with people moved and swayed to his tune. I breathed a sigh of relief and knew that not everything is human. Sometimes, we get an extra revealed miracle from above to make it all happen.

The congregants came, the children were ready, and the Chabad house turned into Rosh Hashanah.

I felt well enough to sit with everyone at the Yom Tov (holiday) meal; I even felt more alive than I did in the past few months. His smile reached mine, and I realized that a silent partner is the blessing every *shlucha* needs.

I sat at the table with happy faces on each side of me. I was reminded, and comforted, that *shlichus* means that the family is in it together, and each one has his or her own part.

Sometimes, *Yiddishe* mamas can lose sight of what is important and right to do. Being a mother, a *shlucha*, and a wife means setting priorities and raising children in the way she wants them to be raised. I respectfully allow my husband to see to my needs and let him step into my inner circle. When I allow him to be the hero for that temporary or extended moment, it goes a long way for all the family members to be at peace.

With just a few kids on my skirt, I imagine that everything is on me, and I must be the one to get it done. Then, with more and more little hands tugging on you, you must understand what is really needed at each little and big moment. It's the way Hashem wants life to work with His master plan behind our untrained eyes.

We can ask ourselves the question, why is this meant to be? Perhaps life really doesn't slow down in the way we imagine it needs to run and function. Yet, it really surprises us and speeds up in the way it's meant to blossom; somehow, everything is where it's meant to be.

These little hands that tug on my skirt are my future, my life, my dreams, my goals, and my ambitions. Their voice is our voice, and I must never get too busy and forget to hear their inner voice.

If I need to be the *Yiddishe* mama, doing what mothers should do and raising their voices to be the next generation, then it's OK to have a new legend, another pair of hands in your kitchen for a short while, or even a semi-permanent while, if that makes things run smoothly.

Sometimes, it's OK to just go with the flow and allow Hashem to show you the real way to live life. It's OK even to let go of the reins in the kitchen, and Hashem will guide you into a better, more meaningful life.

my dear old friend: maintenance

A little extra effort in a Jewish home becomes
rich with flavors, colors, and true peace.

the water from the faucet is sliding fast downwards, and there is a vigorous splish-splash of waterworks on the mountain of dishes before me. I turn around to find myself in the wee early morning hours. I quickly glance at the time, one-thirty: *Ouch! Can it really be so late?*

I just finished cleanup, and the ladies' group will be coming soon. Well, that's not entirely true. First, it will be breakfast for the boys, then Hebrew school, and finally, the ladies will come for our discussion group. So, why am I still up?

It's something I like to call maintenance—keeping everything organized maintains one's post as a *shlucha*, which is the shining star of the greatest symphony when it's done right. Maintenance becomes the needed skill to acquire it.

It is the greatest key to treasure on *shlichus*. Forlorn is the *shlucha* without it; tattered pants, wrinkled shirts, and ink splattered clothes become the horror of abandoning your dear old friend, maintenance.

It appears from the outside that the lives of *shluchim* are perfect. Perhaps, miraculously, we can wave a wand and the rooms clean themselves, but in reality, a few hours of a good Jewish program can take weeks and months to prepare.

When one thinks of "bedtime," is ten at night too late for you? In our world of women emissaries, there is no bedtime until all the work is done, and sometimes that means sleeping just a couple of hours at night.

I like to watch the newcomers, the eyes of perfect strangers that dance around the room. Their gaze touches upon all of the big things, little things, and other things I forgot existed. The newcomer's floating eyes capture the energy of that particular space that was newly entered and kept maintained.

One of the first things one notices is the warmth of their surroundings and the maintenance of that perfectly tidied space. The more effort you put in all the way around, the more people will want to fill that happy space they call the Jewish home.

It transpired early on in our *shlichus* that we had a huge event, and the head *shliach* had acquiesced to our invite. My heart was beating to the tune that every *shlucha* knows too well.

I worked as a good servant to my kitchen and glamoured my cooking style to the highest standard. I hurriedly put the designs and glitz on the tables and tried to beat the clock.

In my haste to reach perfection, I forgot a most treasured but simple detail. I looked around, and everywhere there was a space was now covered with dirty dishes. I covered my mouth in horror; I couldn't believe this silly little (but big) thing that I'd done.

My face burned with a rosy flush, and I felt my embarrassment overwhelm me. It was ten minutes to the program, and what was I to do? I quickly told my husband my embarrassing tale, and he said, "We have no choice. We will block the kitchen and serve everything on the tables."

Somehow my husband always seems to find solutions and give the right answer even when I make silly mistakes. "Okay, that sounds like a great idea," I heard myself mutter.

However, it didn't take long before the door had knocks, creaks, and bangs all of its own. People, including the head *shliach*, wanted and needed to use the kitchen *qvart*—the washing cup. I just stood there and allowed the laughter to pour out of my mouth. Soon after, it came flowing freely and unfiltered in all sizes and shapes.

I was completely mortified and ashamed; I couldn't begin to find the words in a situation like this. I had wanted to impress the newcomers who flooded the house. I had wanted to see all the smiles of the happy customers. Instead, it was imperfect and more disorganized than ever.

Afterward, I paced like I always did when things went wrong, and charts and lists were scribbled down during pauses. It was decided that all preparations must be complete on the day of an event, and the leftover time would be allotted for table decorations. It would be about real solutions that had to be enacted for kitchen maintenance.

How can I practically keep a kitchen clean when there is so much going on and I have so little real help? This is the dose of reality that comes with your dear old friend maintenance: that real help is hard to find. However, before I could even complain, people came to help me out like sprinkled bees in clusters arriving to give back to their community.

Even with the helping hands of ten kind men, there is always something abandoned at the last possible minute. When there is the rush of holidays, Shabbos, and Hebrew school, my dear old friend maintenance comes out of his hiding place once again.

It happened once, when I was figuring out the great mystery of maintenance, that I had happened to be visiting an older friend. She was a courageous woman who had fourteen children of her own.

Now, when your thoughts wander to the idea of fourteen jumping girls and boys, the impressions are such that space will be filled with clutter. There might even be welcome signs of the disorganized piles of forgotten maintenance.

Surprisingly, every spot held itself, and its place sparkled with its own proud tune. "How is this possible?" I wondered out loud in a half muttering, half speaking voice. I started to look around and watched her up close to see what she did and how she beat us all at this game.

One day, I had the courage and found the words to ask her this most personal of questions. It was a question surrounded by mystery and a mother's pride in her key to her home. She replied with an all-knowing smile filled with real solutions.

She told me that "C.A.U.G." is the name of her dear maintenance friend. She then explained that this abbreviation stood for a simple meaning: "Clean As You Go." This made a lot of sense, but it's easier said than done.

We thought to ourselves how hard it would be to clean up after everyone; nevertheless, my husband and I started to implement this "C.A.U.G." rule inside our Chabad house and eventually our own home.

I was so surprised at how much faster and cleaner the atmosphere was as a result of this. Now, when people come over, I don't have to say, "Hold on!" Well, sometimes—just to make sure the kids don't topple people.

Our Chabad house is a place filled with cleanliness and smiles. It's definitely a secret that comes to my mind when I think of "C.A.U.G." A little old lady with fourteen kids and a spotless house comes into my mind and heart.

a friendship of roses laid to rest

Real kindness is when there are no strings attached.

the dreaded phone call and the pledge of responsibility come to the few with the courage to act and perform the greatest kindness for an absolute stranger.

It was an act that entailed purifying the soul, to give it back to its Keeper. A secret society works at all hours with silence between them, and only prayers are found on their lips—the secret prayers of an ancient, holy tongue.

It was about six years into our *shlichus*, and this eerie feeling kept nagging at my conscience. I realized what was bothering me. I had never worked for a *chevra kadisha* (Jewish burial society) before, and my community needed an experienced person to take over for the elders in the society.

I was nervous, for it was a work that no one asks for, and no one can refuse if asked. I tossed and turned at night, knowing that it would soon be my turn to be chosen.

One day, a young girl we knew well in our community had suddenly passed away overnight. They wanted me to watch over the group to ensure everything followed the standards of what needed to be done.

I went regardless of the fear in my gut, a fear of the unknown, and a fear of what I would see. When the time came, and I entered the room, the scene was like it had fallen out of a picture book.

The older ladies took care of the deceased so peacefully and with as much love as only a grandmother could give. It turned out after all that I was needed to fulfill a post which was left vacant in haste. I quickly and quite nervously washed my hands before I joined in the ceremony.

I held tight to my principles to ensure that the process was done according to Jewish law, making everything right for this holy soul. Over time, the group and its leader became closer with me.

I was an outsider who was befriended by a special woman who embraced this *mitzvah* (commandment) of everlasting kindness.

We ended up working quite well together, like a clock tuned to its rightful chime. Time passed, but the feeling of responsibility never did. It was always close to me like a cherished, lost sibling.

The group leader was an older woman who taught me how to respectfully treat one who passed away. Even though I've learned the tools for this great task elsewhere, it was this woman's gentle touch and extreme kindness that made this job feel so special and blessed. We ended up becoming very close, she, the mother of this society, and me, the inheritor.

Our phones were quite often flavored with the spice of love and friendship. The little old lady persisted in getting to know her favorite newcomer of sorts; she wanted to understand my world, life, and views. She was curious about me, a young mother who fought to help souls.

It was a complete shock when she asked me to be the one to lead the burial society. I was flattered but apprehensive about how it would be viewed, this great decision to bring the *Chabad* character to the forefront.

Surprisingly, the other members agreed, feeling that I was the right choice. Who knew an outsider could be chosen to lead a closed group, a special group, a holy group that blessed souls.

Then it happened: my phone calls were not returned, and I felt something was just not right. When my phone rang, there was sobbing on the other end of it. This mother of souls, and leader of the group, was *niftar* (passed away). Now it would be her turn, and she now needed to take her journey back to her Creator.

It was my turn to cry and my choice to sorrowfully and silently grieve as most emissaries do when our congregants have become close to us. I would have to give her, my friend and my mentor, the *taharah* (the ceremony of purifying the dead) and quietly say my goodbyes.

I remembered entering the room, and as I knocked, I felt tears falling down my cheeks. I held my breath when I saw her once vibrant face which had become just an empty shell. Her presence was felt even more than before, and yet I knew when the year of her passing was up, it would lay to rest a friendship of roses.

A familiar scent of understanding washed over me, and I understood that with time, everything would be okay. Unfortunately, it was one of the hardest and saddest things that I ever had to do. However, it was a great privilege to take care of this legend: a mother of souls.

As I finished my work and quietly closed the door, I felt a sense of peace and pride wash over me; from now on, I would have to be the teacher and take care of the *taharahs*. As I walked to my car, I cherished even more each day of living and spending time with family.

a roller coaster ride that never ends

It's a ride that cannot be stopped unless the passenger becomes the driver; only then will the chaos, and the ride, be in your hands.

the bumps and turns of one rollercoaster ride ends, and as one touches her feet to the ground, she finds herself sitting again on another ride, a greater ride, and this ride turns one in all directions.

I entered the doors of my small but great house, and the children ran to me, half-crying and half-laughing. With the keys still dangling in the door, I embrace them all, and I carefully lift the newest member of our family above the chaos and into his little bed.

It will be the first and last day of another pair of hands; as my friend was leaving that day, the emotional ups and downs begin. I start with baby steps, one small, teeny step at a time. Slowly, my kids believe me that two days away in the hospital means Mommy is coming back again, and she is not leaving forever!

The hugs, outbursts, crying, screaming, and laughing enveloped them with the atmosphere of hugs and a gentleness so fine that I needed to pinch myself to acknowledge it's me. Sometimes, it's hard to be so patient. Sometimes, I can lose the challenge and fail; patience is the true gift that one can give to a growing family's needs.

There is deep frustration with every spoon and chair out of place. Then I realize that I must let go and allow a deep sigh—I can be imperfect for a few weeks. The situation that really matters is that one is calm and joyful; the kids live and breathe around their mother in her aura of a kind light.

A few days after birth, I was faced with the reality that each step will be a long one, that I needed to take it down many notches, let the organized status quo be, and allow things to be imperfect! The idea was to rise above the here and now: to appreciate each little and big moment with one's diamonds, her children, even when it appears like the opposite was staring one in the face.

As we pull up to the driveway and sit there in the car, the realization hits me that the biggest helper I have is ten years old! With seven kids, this is a big moment for me to take in. The next morning, I make a great effort to go down the stairs to help and be with the family because my friend and helper will be leaving tomorrow morning!

There is nothing to keep her here except my fear of doing it all alone right after a brand-new baby. She sees me participating with her and laughing with my children, and she takes this as a sign that all is well, and all will be well.

My mind knows she is right, but my heart wants her to stay and make everything feel relaxed and comfortable again—like before the rollercoaster.

As time settles, and one's post is not so lonely anymore, the people come in all sizes and shapes to be there for me, their *rebbetzin*. Then it becomes easier to fall back into the routine of things and go beyond what's being needed or asked of me.

The kids follow happily along because each little task given to them is cherished as part of the family's needs. This is especially done for its responsibility and shared as a group effort, but there is no perfect plan or recipe that will make it all work out after another birth.

Perhaps, last time was different, and this time it's meant to be better, but the rewards are clearer to me. It also becomes a time when the family and community must come along for the bumpy ride because becoming the driver and not a passenger goes a long way.

As lights to our community, everyone expects our hands to lift them out of their hardships. It's our words that embrace them and heal them, but what remains forgotten is us. It is the sacrifice of living so far away from our own community, family, and friends that make things harder than they need to be. We always choose to dance around each person in need, but this causes the curtains to go down on our own needs.

How can I, the *rebbetzin*, the comforter to many, demand helpers of my own? It should be obvious to the onlooker that I need help and so does my family.

We are grateful to those who roll up their sleeves and pitch in, and for those who don't, we always choose not to judge them. When the help leaves, it then becomes a long walk to the finish line.

People use "my spouse" as an expression. People think of one's spouse as their own, but my spouse is not just mine or my children's, he belongs almost equally to the community. One can even argue that he belongs more to the community than to me! Therefore, he must keep doing his part undistracted, even if he wants to stay and help out.

The nighttime feedings for our newest member and early breakfast for the family become a challenge only for me. Although my spouse helps with many things—laundry, dishes, and the Mr. Fun aspect at the home front—the main stability rests with me and me alone.

My good energy and smile keep the mood going for everyone, including me. If the towel is thrown in, and I allow myself to be the passenger on the roller coaster ride, then I lose, and the whole family falls into that trap together with me.

The family sits down, and all the little ones' contributions make it well worth each moment invested. The stories told of Chabad *Chassidim* and their hardships, so long ago, focus us on living our lives better. We realize this moment of difficulty will pass, or perhaps it's not a bad moment at all but just another great lesson learned.

Maybe, one just needs to open one's eyes to the reality of the glass half full. Then the possibility of a life-changing moment is more real than the little tumbles of mess and worry.

misjudged

Not every moment that doesn't go as planned is wrong.

We want things to fit into our own imaginings. We feel angry when the gift wrapping of what we want doesn't fall in our direction. Sometimes, when we think a little bigger and misjudge a little less, the purpose becomes clearer.

The time stood still with what felt like the sun walking shyly behind the moon. The days seemed to change just for us while we waited impatiently for real answers.

It was a bitter place in what resembled an empty life. It seemed that all of our dreams—our life ambitions—were crushed forever. The unknown worrying, wondering, and obsessing were a mistake, but the helplessness and hurting inside didn't mind their companions.

It was over! The last place was not for us, and now, we'd traveled to places and places but there was no string of luck. It was like an emotional rollercoaster, and our hearts grew weary from this endless waiting.

We were tired out; we decided that this would be the last turn before a break was needed. We finally arrived at what we had hoped was our last destination.

It was a huge mansion, beautiful and well worn. The dated, old, wooden walls made the mansion appear friendly and familiar. I sat back in my chair, hoping that this interview would be different than the long line of what had been before.

The meeting started, and a graying, middle-aged rabbi began the meeting in a commanding tone. The mood was a bit too serious for my taste, and questions were thrown around like a game of darts gone wrong.

I started thinking, "What can I do? Can I change the hyped-up serious tone? Can I have an impact? Do I even want to fight for this place?" These questions were nagging at me until I had a chance to make a move.

I finally stepped in with some statements of my own. I had to make a dent, so that without a doubt or a question it would be clear that we were special and not to be glossed over and shut out: "He is not the regular rabbi you meet. You don't know my husband. You don't know how incredibly talented and brilliant he is."

I knew that I must have sounded like an out of sync clown or a cheerleader. However, I saw the writing on the wall, and it didn't look good. We were strangers to him, so what would make us the right choice when others waited to be interviewed?

The graying rabbi held a matter-of-fact tone etched into his persona with an added seasoning of nervous zeal that we were unlucky to receive. It didn't help that he preferred to stand up as he grew more excited in his line of questioning.

This round, he turned his attention to me and said, "You still seem so sad about the last position. Are you ready to move on and have a new one?"

I thought about his words, and I thought about when we first went to our last post. The excitement and energy were our breath and life for our tired limbs in our first few months. The hard work never ended, and the nine-to-five was a breeze compared to the long work weeks that we pulled off. Yet, even with big dark circles under tired eyes, we were more alive than ever.

It felt like icy freezing water was being splashed over our faces, when the surreal understanding of what had happened hit us.

When we realized that the hard-earned home was not for us but would be for another, we felt this nagging pain-filled bitterness that welded deeply with our confused minds. What went wrong?

It would be a steep, hard climb to look for a new place that would be right for us. I wish we would've known the right place from the wrong one. It could've been a much less emotional journey, but sometimes it is only through difficulty and struggle that one becomes a leader.

The journey of searching and the gentle letdowns by the rabbis that we'd encountered were difficult. Our waiting became our grief and hope for the tomorrow that would finally come.

My thoughts had settled themselves, and I looked up to give my collected response. I took a deep breath and pushed my emotions off to the sidelines, for they had no place in this room. I finally gave my reply, "The answer to your question is that I am more than ready to begin a new *shlichus*."

He looked at us with those serious, stern eyes and wished us a good day. Now began the wait to see if there would be another interview. It was a short few weeks later, and the rabbi that was interviewing us decided that he wanted to wait.

At the time, I was devastated. What went wrong? This feeling crept up on me that this wasn't the last time we would see him. Perhaps, we were just a number like so many others. Sure enough, we were interviewed by him again and given a few positions to choose from. However, our hearts found a place a little further away.

As life moved on and our second *shlichus* became super successful, we, as a family, became close with this stern rabbi, who became less severe as time went on. He and my husband even became good friends. Then, with even more time that passed, he became part of our extended family.

When I look back at my first impressions of this rabbi, it was obvious to me that I had misjudged him. It is easy to react to people in haste and pull out different blame cards when things take a wrong turn.

It is so easy to tragically misjudge a person's actions and behavior. Our path forward can have many turns with twists, but how we react to a situation is up to us.

the battle of the spouses

Real winning is transforming war into peace.

it was loud, filled with machines running and workers feeling the sweat and heat from an over-packed meat plant.

A woman, heavily pregnant with her eyes unfocused, sat on a stool lost in thought. As an adult, she felt conflicted, and brewed with regret. She remembered as a little girl being stuck in these problematic family experiences.

It threw her into the unknown and unfamiliar healthy family lifestyle because she was too familiar with chaos and war. How could she raise up her own house? She felt too tired to fight but couldn't find the right choices to help herself and her family. All the hand-me-downs of her parents' influence turned into a home filled with bad decisions that ended negatively.

A man, her husband, is forced to stand for hours with no choice as he watches the meat-packing lines. He, too, fades into his memories of rough times. Many of the situations he fell into as a child hadn't mended themselves.

He remained bitter about it and struggled to move forward. He wanted the dream—the dream of being a family, united, and at peace with one another. Unfortunately, that idea seemed long gone, and he felt like he was slipping into his own parents' messy mistakes.

Yet, it was all he ever knew and all he chose to know. There was no hope to step outside of it, and it trailed behind him like a nudge. The nudge bumped into him on his most important choices, and he couldn't find the right mindset to set the nudge straight.

A few hours passed, and it was break time for most of the workers. She sat on her chair to watch the work be completed. It seemed to her that something was amiss. Lunch time came and went, but that day no lunch was to be had.

What happened, she wondered? Where was lunch? She sat with her husband together in the workplace, having again left her lunch at home and depending on her husband to pick up what she neglected to do.

The spouses' battle continued on its journey, and this couple found no peace with one another, and no trust. The husband's long hours were taking their toll, and the husband decided today he didn't want to bring her lunch, and his very pregnant wife could figure it out another way.

A friend of this couple, a mother of one of the toddlers in my program, came to see me in secret. She nervously admitted to me that her friend was having trouble at home. Her friend was heavily pregnant, going to work, and had no food to eat. Could I please help her?

As I stepped away, the conversation continuously sat on my shoulders, and even with a deep concern for my fellow, I forced myself to be busy again. Her words, though, clung to me like static, and I could find no rest until I got to the bottom of this.

I have my rules, and usually, I only would let couples and families hang out with us in the Chabad house because our own house is the children's space to be themselves. However, we wanted to connect more with this particular family, and I decided to invite them to our home, even if that meant that we would be sharing the children's space for a time.

This family was a misfit from the start. It was her second marriage at all of twenty-one, and his third marriage being all of thirty-one. They tried hard to make the impossible possible and blend themselves as one unit even with the ten-year age difference and coming together from broken homes.

They now had a few children on their laps, and their kids were very close to their hearts. Help was needed to try to stop the battle of the spouses and make sure this couple could win the war of peace.

It became the routine to have marriage counseling in our house each week to smooth out the bumps. If my kids were playing in a room and the couple wanted the space because it looked like the right place to have a conversation, I would then move all the kids, toys, and snacks to let them have it.

It was definitely hard on my kids to be constantly transferred from room to room because they were all so little, but I knew how important it was to be flexible to help this couple save their marriage.

The children and I had to be creative to go elsewhere and give them the space they needed, and it helped the tone and level of excitement of the kids to quiet down.

After each meeting, it felt like the couple, both of them, were even angrier at each other. It was like they took turns in this battle that never seemed to end. If one was happy and smiled, then you knew the other was simply seething and miserable. They took the family counseling session as a time and place to make fun of each other and bring up each fault as if reading off a long shopping list that kept on going.

My husband was excellent at counseling others and usually achieved a great outcome, but here he was refereeing them like a coach would on a sports team. All the time, he felt like a referee and was constantly changing up his approach as to how to handle this couple that apparently liked war and not peace.

One week the couple had a major fight, and his young wife decided that she wanted to teach her husband a lesson. So, she contacted a few girls who abhorred her husband and loved playing their own war at home. The night was set, and she walked out of the house with the children to sleep elsewhere.

After a long day at work, her husband came home to an unlocked door and no one to greet him. No note, no text, no phone call—just the whispers of what could have happened.

"Is everything alright? Where are the children, and where is my wife?" the man thought worriedly and became restless with fear.

Meanwhile, at her friend's house, she inconvenienced the host in her haste to teach her husband a lesson. Her unsettled, confused children were taking over the hysterics, and her constant need for reassurance that she was right, and her husband was wrong, made the night that much harder.

The couple who was hosting her began feeling very uncomfortable, and later they found themselves knee-deep in a fight that they wanted no part of.

The host kept telling her to call her husband to let him know that she was safe. She flat out refused, arguing that her husband needed to beg her to come back. Well, she ended up staying there the whole night, and it did nothing to help an already shaky marriage.

The husband's fear of what could have occurred turned to anger and embarrassment, and he chose not to beg her to come home, even though the host graciously let him know the family was safe.

Time passed and the argument faded, but the memory clung close to them like a ringing alarm clock. They then again came for Shabbos, and things seemed to be going well for a time. They would laugh, smile with each other, and it was almost forgotten that they were usually knee-deep in disagreements.

Then, on Shabbos afternoon, I got a loud knock on my door. She was crying and begging me to let her come inside. I quickly let her in and put my husband in charge of the children. I then offered her tea and some cookies, hoping that it could be a productive conversation.

She sat quietly eating for a second but then said hysterically, crying as cookies, tea, and tears spilled out, "My husband is a bad man, a very bad man."

Hearing words like this, you cannot help but think of the worst possible things. Even though you keep reminding yourself of the source from where these words are coming from. It was at most just a tit for tat between the two of them.

After much discussion, it became clear that they had another battle of the spouses, and when she lost the round of disagreements, it made her feel awful. She then liked to tell as many people as possible that her spouse was a terrible, horrible human being.

I thought to myself, when will this nonsense end? When will it be not about the tit for tat or current battle, but the overall picture? What do they want in their house, constant war or peace?

It's not about keeping score and getting back at each other; it's about the relationship and the home that's being created. If the children see happy faces, peaceful interactions, a wife being a hostess, and a husband being the host, then they learn how to be good people.

Slamming doors and screaming at one another won't keep a home at peace, and the children grow up hurt, wounded, and afraid to leap into marriage themselves. The child battles their feelings of "If Mommy and Daddy can't make it, then how can I?"

After a few years of working with this couple each week, it seemed that much progress had been made, and the need for them to remain a family became more important than the need for drama and arguments.

So, it looks like, for now, they both are taking the peaceful road. It might have plenty of hiccups and holes along the way, but at least it's in the right direction.

Perhaps, if most couples can react kindly, care for, and respect one another, peace can illuminate the home, and one spouse will follow the example of the other. The battles and small wars can finally disappear, and a week can go by without the need for drama.

When one lets the big picture be the guide, staying calm and allowing true happiness to seep in, then the family is winning the ultimate war, and for the next generation, it will be whole, complete, and a brand-new peaceful chapter.

the impact of choices

When you're inspired, just go for it!

my whole life's goals and dreams were flying around like feathers in the wind, circling my clouded head. The songs of purpose and faith that I sang and absorbed each summer for over almost two decades were to be laid aside for tomorrow's generation.

Our path ahead remained like uncharted waters, and this mystery held our excitement, but it was tempered with worry and fear. The deep recesses of my mind began to nag at me, and I questioned my faith in *shlichus*: Is this time going to be different?

To stand up and choose such a life of service can feel heroic and exceptional, but the truth is, it has many hardships that come sewn in the pockets of leadership.

When we went out on our first *shlichus*, it was such an incredible feeling to be finally helping out Jewish people in our little shul. Unfortunately, as time crawled by, it became crystal clear that the *shlichus* was not very suited for us, and sadly, we had to move on and find our rightful place elsewhere.

When one comes to this heartbreaking conclusion, it becomes a time of reflection and extreme pain, as if it were the sea's splitting. Each place suits each couple like a glove to its rightful hand. Sadly, our first place didn't work out, and now it was time to move on.

I remember that it was just after I'd had my second child, and we found ourselves rethinking our mission in life. This first *shlichus* didn't work out. Did we still want to do a life's service for humankind?

The very idea of going out and giving up the luxuries of life is beyond the usual, and it is not what most people want to do. Most people would prefer that another person should gift-wrap all his needs and desires and place them inside the perfect basket of life's comforts.

I enjoy the perfect basket too, but for me, this was the only way life could be: to be a giver. I grew up on *shlichus* and couldn't understand how not to live a life of service. The pain of knowing that I might never be a giver or leader again was enormous for me.

I kept tormenting myself with the same questions: Will the impact of my choices change the mission that I hold so dear? It was useless to think of a different tomorrow when I knew my heart had only one dream and one purpose.

Each day, I woke up to the in-betweens of life, pacing back and forth in our small apartment. It became difficult that instead of running around and sharing warmth, my world became a darkened place, and I held no candle to illuminate fresh light.

My routine was no longer mine and definitely not the same. The unknown in our day, week, or month became our serious decisions in life that felt like they were dangling on a bent key chain.

I had to distract myself from my nagging thoughts of what our fate would be: *Shlichus* or no *shlichus*? I had no choice, so I forced myself to get up and started getting busy with different kinds of volunteer work and a regular job.

It was summertime, and a nice friend offered me a camp-counselor job for little kids. My happiness and excitement for this newfound work breathed new life into me. The old, mundane energy strayed behind as an afterthought. The pace picked up, and I was thrown into a world of movement. I quickly rolled up my sleeves to leap into the new acceleration.

My friend wanted me to invest my energies into this well-established camp, and even though I loved teaching and directing the children, I decided that it would take too much energy to invest in this project. The time needed to be spent focusing on moving on and finding our new *shlichus*.

The feeling of flying and living again was short-lived, and I had to busy myself with new things, so I started taking my kids on walks and inviting people for my husband to tutor. As each day passed and more interviews fell to the ground, our journey as a family became like a carriage on a rickety unpaved road.

In the interim, I felt we were less a part of the group and more like the wanderers left behind. We stood there with others who could not turn the corner from being a leader of humanity to being absorbed into the regular community.

When we mingled with these wanderers, they, in turn, shared with us their painful tales of abandoned missions. Unaware of a general's difficult post, people began to mock and even belittle the significant trials and victories won by the Rebbe's soldiers.

A tragedy shook the world and restored its faith in the Rebbe's *shluchim*. Journalists kept replaying what they, the *kedoshim* (holy ones who were murdered), symbolized: they held no need for the physical, all they needed was a small place to live because they gave everything of themselves for others and expected nothing in return.

The *kedoshim* (holy ones), the rabbi and *rebbetzin* of Mumbai, were a pair of angel doves that went out to take hold of one of the earth's darkest places. In their tiresome journey, they held and kept the promise of creating a home for G-d.

It was a tragedy that made us hold our breath for hope, and it was sadly not meant to be. We watched the screen and fiddled with the radio, but all was in vain because the angel of death had come to collect his most precious of bundles; Hashem (G-d) came to take them back home.

As I got to know the *shlucha* (a woman emissary), more in death than in life itself, I realized her incredible strengths on all fronts; hers was a trial of faith, and on every corner, her heels crossed over that threshold.

It happened that night more so than any other night, and she peaked in the ultimate test of self-sacrifice. It was then that her courage and bravery were shown to all.

It was the story of her self-sacrifice that stoked the fire within me to hold myself upright and proudly go out once again. The odds were against us succeeding, but I knew that we had to go out and do the work that the *kedoshim* laid out for us commoners.

It was to embrace the love; it was a concern touched by angels, which we realized had set the bar fifty feet higher than ever before. The bar held us to super standards of great inspiration. It pushed us to travel to a place far from our own comfort, and we then chose to be a comfort to many.

b'dieved

B'dieved is a situation that is not preferred
but forced due to circumstance.

it was Erev Pesach (the eve of Passover), and each step was carefully
planned out as I ran around trying to make it all somehow happen.
Pesach (Passover) cleaning is taking its sweet old time, and my *gan*, the
homeschool classroom, is pressuring the students to produce real fruit.

A phone call is made, and my shoulders are overburdened with one
more unsuspected load—the burden and *mitzvah* (commandment) of
taking care of a *mes* (dead person). I found myself not in the mood for
this *mitzvah*, with no one to help me this Erev Pesach with such a delicate and meaningful task.

I would be alone, and to begin with, it would be *b'dieved*. *B'dieved* refers
to a situation that forces one to do an act of holiness not in the preferred
way. A problem was that there were not enough people, so I would have
to use another way to start. I always tried to make each encounter special—with each person, dead or alive—to let them know I cared.

My phone became busy again, but sadly no one stepped forward to
join the burial society. Each person had her reasons, and it was all on
my shoulders now.

As time moved forward, my mood started to change based on my
excitement over helping, even though I knew it was *b'dieved*.

The transformation of energy that filled the air became electric;
I anticipated the great opportunity I had to fulfill this *mitzvah*, and gone
was my moment of sadness.

No matter what the circumstance, I decided that it would be a labor of love and faith enveloped together. I would humble myself and allow Hashem (G-d) to guide me in what He had in store.

I said hello to the caretaker and his helpers. Their smiles were not plastered on; they were exploding for real. I thought to myself that it must get lonely in a funeral home. Perhaps, my interactions give them tall tales to talk about, and I bring the circus inside the quiet, eerie doors.

On *shlichus*, I was expecting again, and I was the only female representative of the *chevra kadisha* (burial society) for miles around. I was desperately looking for little helpful tidbits to focus myself with the right intentions before I began the *taharah*, a service of purity for a *mes*.

I knocked to show *kavod* (honor and respect) for the deceased, and I was quickly pulled aside by the caretaker. He looked at me worriedly and said words that one in the midst of holy work abhors hearing: "Excuse me! She is contagious, and you need a mask."

"What?" I stood back, alarmed, unsure of what to do. I've never taken care of a contagious dead person before. I was pregnant and forced to embrace a difficult and uncomfortable situation.

It was then explained to me that I would need all the works for this delicate endeavor. Out came the mask, apron, heavy-duty gloves, and of course, worried looks.

This time I knocked again. Gone was the intimate and *heimishe* (warm and relaxed) feeling of family that I always would reserve to embrace this commandment and take care of the deceased so carefully. Absent and forlorn was the long, drawn-out ritual and the humming of tunes so pleasantly sung with precision, as work was honorably done with love.

It was a situation forced from grace to instead become *b'dieved*, and even worse, the deceased would lose some special parts of the *taharah* (service of purity) itself—a piece of my heart experienced brokenness from being cuffed and forced to hasten a service. Instead of a special time of the burial society ritual, it became replaced by a *b'dieved* purification, full of worry and fear.

This time the work had to be done super meticulously, almost robotically, and with much haste. Each droplet of water that touched the flesh had to be laboriously protected. Holy water had to cover the deceased, and the words were said in a voice of worry and extreme focus.

I was ashamed of how I was reacting. My task was being done with fear, not respect. The *mes*, her soul that hovers over until she is buried, would sense my hurried manner, and not feel embraced by my service. It felt like the situation brought circles and circles of nerves that took turns as I worked to do this job right.

My hands shook a bit as comfortable work felt like a step in the past, because I was now knee-deep in unfamiliar preparations. So, my *b'di-eved* mentality began to take over, and with a heavy sigh, the tedious tasks began.

First came the prayers, then cleaning, washing, *taharah*, and shrouds. Finally, I was ready to place her inside of her resting place. A box so empty and plain was soon filled with a woman kept of memories: a mother, wife, daughter, sister, and friend.

All of her happy times and sad times too were now to be closed off from the world of the living and to be placed into the world of the dead. The last prayers are said, and the door to her box was closed. Psalms were read at her casket, and a candle was placed and lit; draped over her box was the Star of David.

Goodbye and good luck is murmured to her in the holy tongue before her door is closed, and the ceremony becomes a whisper of what once was. It was meant for her to be crossing over to a familiar but old world: a world of new souls, old souls, and souls that wait to go down once more.

the bearer of bad news

Sometimes we have to be the bearer of bad news
and should have the decency to do it gently.

in our lives as emissaries, we are fortunate to come across people from all walks of life. It's like spinning a dreidel where one has the chance to land on the lucky *gimmel* (the third letter of the Hebrew alphabet). Not every encounter is a story of thankfulness with a picture-perfect ending of faith, love, and reform.

Sometimes, years of effort are invested, and with lots of luck, a smile is the whipped-cream reward for a hard-earned dessert.

It happened once that we were privileged to get an invitation from an elderly couple to come to visit them. It was a two-hour drive with a car full of excited and eager boys. Their little noses pressed against the glass for a better view of the repetitive picture of nature.

Along the way, we got creative, pointing emphatically out the window and saying, "Wow, look! There is a tree! There is a cow!" Never mind that this was the hundredth tree or cow we passed. Still, the amusement of kids is their innocent encounter with each little and big thing that they find.

The smiles of the car ride for me are the curious and entertaining moments that we share; as the car bumps and jolts along the road, the children's heads bob up and down, and their eyes pop wide open.

The excitement is all to catch a small, little glimpse of the familiar painting that slides along the outdoors. Thankfully, it calms them down before we enter the elderly couple's house.

The older man's speaking and the little old lady's fiddling became the boys' music as they got busy building puzzles. He tells us of his journey towards G-d, about the Torah scroll that he studies, and his great haste in recovering all his lost time for learning Torah.

Our ears and hearts are full of joy, inspired by a wandering Jew who has found his way home. The next time we visit, the conversations turn more serious—and heartbreaking.

His wife is stuck, frozen in time. It's a prison assigned to many who take a great leap of faith, but the jump is too big for them to take. It happens when they realize they have been tricked out of their greatest wish and dream in life: to be a lifetime member of the Jewish faith.

They asked us in shame, begging for answers, for truth. Can this really be? Was it a huge mistake or perhaps a misunderstanding that has gone wrong? What did we really think or know of what went wrong, and can we share this truth with them of their tortured new reality?

The harsh, bitter reality was finding out that his wife was not converted according to Jewish law, and therefore, all of his children and grandchildren were not Jewish. A 3,300-year-old tradition and chain that was never broken became completely shattered with an honest mistake of the unknowing.

We sat together at their small table, and her friendly persona and *heimishe* (easy-going) personality made their reality that much worse for me. I held her hand tightly, and she felt comfortable crying to me; this sweet old lady broke my heart. She was such an amazing person, and I wanted to help her to overturn her grief, but it was too late to change the outcome of her choices.

Our eyes met theirs in a room full of sacred old books. We looked around, guiding ourselves to the correct answer. There must be honesty as well as a comfort for a beautiful collection of broken dolls—this beautiful but broken couple. There were books everywhere, and a big Torah scroll stood as the guardian in the center of its circle.

Well, if that didn't put pressure on us for an answer, then I don't know what did. Our head *shliach* (emissary) was right; he was honest even when it was extremely uncomfortable. He told this couple long ago that she was not Jewish; therefore, their children were not either, and her only option was to convert again according to Torah law.

One could think, do we play politically correct? "No" is my immediate answer! The main point is to be honest with them and be a mensch. We needed to consider their feelings, to put ourselves in their shoes, and to imagine their lives.

As a couple, they were devastated, their dreams shattered with their family unit broken into what could have been. They had three children that were grown and who also had children themselves.

What would they do? She couldn't turn back time and was not ready to commit to being a full-fledged Jew. All we can do as *shluchim* is to be their comfort and friend in a time of need, to be a shoulder to cry on, and to hold them upright.

Perhaps, with time they will find comfort, peace, and happiness once again. She might turn the hard corner and take the more difficult path, or she might choose not to, but that would be her decision.

To become a convert is not so easy, and definitely not so simple. It's meant to be full of trials and tests, and only the strongest of people who desire to be part of the Jewish nation can leap into a brand-new life. One then immerses in holy waters and becomes reborn, revealing their Jewish soul within.

This couple's story ends with her and her children still not Jewish and with them not planning to convert. Her husband spends his days learning Torah and knows that his line of Judaism ends with him.

Some days, it bothers him more than others, but at least he knows the truth, and sometimes the truth hurts, but that too is part of *shlichus*—to deal with the happy stories and the sad.

It never is an easy job to be the bearer of bad news, but sometimes that is part of the job as *shluchim*.

tiptoeing around
the bigwig

A person can change no matter what the age.

choices become confused; the color gray paints itself on every white page. When people choose to do wrong and appease others, then the color black covers the right choice instead of white. The desire to be understood by the seventy nations seems more important than the law. Like a bride lost in the woods who sees a castle of comforts but gets confused and chooses the peddlers' cottage, so too can our lives become topsy-turvy, and we think that what's wrong is right, and what's right is wrong.

It was our newlywed time with *shlichus* and we were literally walking on tiptoes. Like a juggler at his first show, each move makes an impression, impacting the little worlds of the people you meet.

In a short while, I met a big *macher,* a person that the community held in high respect. The imprint of her impact on others was that of a true *balabusta,* she was known to be a no-nonsense hostess. A famous phrase comes to mind: "A woman of valor, who can find."

Unfortunately, our short dance with friendship never really got off the ground, it became a rather interesting relationship between the two of us. To make it clear, there was definitely tiptoeing going on, and it was strictly from my side. On the other hand, my husband became her favorite rabbi, and I became her person with "no box," meaning she didn't know where to place me.

The deeper reason I sensed her dislike was due to what I stood for: the religious feminist. As a secular woman, she believed that being called to the Torah was a Divine right, and it was her only way to express a meaning of freedom and to bring her voice to center stage.

What she didn't yet realize is that in Judaism, the woman is always at center stage. The Jewish woman is called the foundation of the home, an "*akeres habayis*."

At first, the big *macher* didn't know us that well, and my husband wasn't her favorite rabbi. It had started with a phone call that I had made to her. Once on the phone with her, she said, "What do you really want from me?"

She is a straight shooter, so I laughed nervously and said to her, "It's simple, please can you come to my husband's class and bring your friends."

I couldn't believe my chutzpah, or perhaps it was her straightforwardness that I asked her to come in such a way. So, from that day forward, she came unannounced with her friends tagging along. They came weekly to my husband's class, and she never looked back.

After a few years and then some, there was a sudden surprise in store for me, and she started coming to my book club and ladies' programs. She was an active participant, with wit, sarcasm, and a regality about her that made people want to hang on to her every word. Now, at eighty-five years old, she has slowed down, but definitely we know I have not found her a box, and she has not found one for me yet.

Recently, she has started greeting me in a grandmotherly way. Perhaps, we've grown accustomed to each other, or maybe the Torah way has finally begun to grow on her. Whatever the reason for this most treasured change, it was well worth the wait.

As the years become filled with more knowledge, it then leads a person to the real truth. Her dedication to preserving what once was didn't come with such a feeling of urgency as before.

Torn between the truth of Torah law and dear friends of old, her mind makes compromises for both. Most days, truth is walking beside her, and the old misconceptions of freedoms are lagging quietly behind her.

In our relationship today, the idea of "no box" to us is now being unexpected and breaking the mold of what's expected. As a reform *macher*, the person that the community respects coming weekly to Chabad, she is crossing through many boxes, and it then becomes an honor to appoint her with no box.

At times, the pressure to fit in can be a dangerous weapon, so we must conform to be the pauper and not the prince. It is the price our nation had to pay for with a simple quote, "I'm a Jew in my heart."

It was a hard time for our people, and they were in denial about the Torah's being the real book of the law. She came from a Reform background, and we both passed over many boundaries and have a great relationship today, me being a Chabad *rebbetzin* and her being a reform *macher*. If luck permits, the feminist might find her way towards real truth.

a sisterhood of helpers

A room was ready for its gem and already filled
with prayer and modesty.

the day can stand beautiful and quickly turn dark with the deepest
fog, and the night embraces its peak of blackness, only shortly to turn
into the rainbow of light. It's not enough for Hashem (G-d) that you
pray and then move on in your little station called life. He wants to be
remembered in each big and little moment that He creates.

The light seeped into the room, and dawn flushed out the last touch
of the night. A morning's decision had come at last. This day was the
day a new soul would be welcomed into the world. I wondered which
lucky soul would I greet and meet. I was so excited, with many months
of eagerly waiting for this birth. As a mother of six sons, I wondered if
I would be gifted with another son, or perhaps a first daughter.

As we entered the hospital, we were greeted by the overseer, my
Jewish doctor. He sat there almost hidden from sight with nurses
swarming him and prepping their stations. My eyes looked around the
room, and there I saw my dear friend: the labor coach. Her face lit up
with recognition, for she had found us at last.

She then took hurried steps to embrace me. My nerves, for that split
second, vanished completely. I realized that as much of a planner as I am,
G-d had already put His spin on my story with His holy touch. I just had
to trust Him and let go and allow this day to truly begin.

My doula and I turned a few more corners and passed empty bas-
sinets separated by a piece of glass. I was hoping to get a glimpse of

someone else's story to encourage myself to wait for my own, but the sheets remained untouched.

We then entered the room, and it was how I remembered it. I was back to imagining the six times I gave birth before, each time with the same worry: What will be? The choice was not mine as to when, but I needed to step down and welcome the time I would spend waiting. My loyal doula stood beside me, and this marathon-like routine lay ahead of us.

Pacing the long hospital hallways and getting lost in conversation, we turned a corner, and I purposely avoided the nurses' station. My friend asked me the reason for this, and I said it was for modesty.

I must have looked ridiculous walking around wearing two hospital gowns and still avoiding the public station. However, I knew that even in labor, modesty must not be cast aside. Instead, it must be the main torch to this day's completion.

It seemed more than an hour had passed, so we carefully made our way back to the room. We were greeted by the rabbi of our community, my husband of twelve years. He had come to help us with his job as well.

He gifted everyone with a suitcase full of jokes and good-felt messages of humor. One joke after another was said, perfectly timed to make me laugh and smile and forget for the moment of what lay ahead.

Then, in the midst of jokes and laughter, the nurse turned to me and said, "I think I need to call the S.W.A.T. team." My husband and I looked at each other and excitedly remarked, "We've been here before. It's the only way to get the needle in my arm." Soon the Pitocin (hormone to induce labor) was given, and it then slowly began its mission of labor.

The door continued to be swung open like a breezy window that was never properly shut. The nurses had heard I was a seventh-time mom, and their uniforms whistled with movement.

The shy but eager smiles were coming from a team of baby nurses all anticipating the moment's arrival, or so they thought. They worked quickly and carefully, for the preparation had finally begun, and little lights were turned on. The baby's table was being set up. My heart was beating with excitement that something was finally happening, until another, and then another hour passed.

My friend and midwife had made her apologies for lateness, and almost as if we were at a coffee shop, we began to talk about life. Here we were, a Muslim, Lutheran, and a Jew, all set on caring for the next generation to come.

I sat on my huge birth ball as we spoke at length about religion, custom, modesty, and faith until my doula jokingly interrupted, "I don't hear a woman in labor." I laughed but then felt concerned. It was almost *shkiah* (dusk), and there was still no sign of our most important guest.

There was a loud knock, and my sisterhood of helpers all peeked into the doorway. The loud voice at the door boomed with excitement that one Jew had for another during their time of *simchah* (a joyous occasion).

The Jewish doctor was eagerly looking to congratulate the rabbi. He was shocked when I said that he was unwelcome to enter my room at this time, and the rabbi is home with his sons but will be back soon.

It was late at night, the halls seemed empty of visitors, and smiley faces of encouragement were long gone. They were now replaced with a deep quietness that forced me to focus more inwards as each next step was taken.

It was my duty now to do whatever I could to enable the transition for the baby from one world to the next. Each hour that passed by felt more urgent than the last. This preparation was more about making sure everything on our side was done properly for this soul's new holy beginning.

We paced the long halls again, this time with my doula on one side of me and my midwife on the other. Every few steps, I would hunch over and hold my doula's hand. She looked at me with this knowing look that soon, the dark fog of the unknown would end, and we would begin again on a new journey.

Somehow, the holding of my friend's hand and the pat on the back from my midwife refocused my mind and helped my exhausted, achy limbs to continue to do their job.

Their powerful and very human touch and embrace ruled out the fear and worry of the storm. The gentle whispering of kind words of this great sisterhood eased my pain and sent waves of comfort to the unborn child within.

After much difficulty, we head back cautiously to see if progress was made. Finally, there was a turn in my story; it was time for a beautiful soul to enter our little room—a room that was ready for its gem and already filled with prayer and modesty.

The sisterhood of helpers surrounded my bed, and a loud cry was heard at last! I lifted my eyes to see a shiny new face declaring his fire to our world. After six beautiful boys, a seventh light was added that night.

My husband was then welcomed into the room and held his brand-new son. My mother-in-law followed shortly afterward, and the room was dancing its own song of pure jubilation. This journey was finished and completed, and the next journey was finally just beginning.

the boy who didn't let him die alone

Breaking a bad habit is hard.

the fight, the struggle—to a troubled old man, the situation was so real and difficult, and nonetheless, he couldn't stop his drinking. He was all alone and surrounded by good memories, sad memories, and memories he wished he could forget.

Some days he felt like a tornado: out of control, like he just couldn't stop. An addictive, terrible old habit, he sadly couldn't quit. Each night, he begged and pleaded with his Creator: "Just one more chance, and I'll make it alright; tomorrow, I promise to be better!"

His kids, his friends, his wife all pleaded and even begged him to change. It was chance after chance with little change that forced Hashem's (G-d) hand to keep the door of mercy closed but unlocked, or so those who knew him imagined it to be.

Alone with bedsores, his conflicted memories, and the trouble that consumed his days, he became a forgotten, old, worn-out man stuck in a nursing home, and his room became empty and neglected, with only his rabbi to greet him each week.

However, this determined, fallen man knew G-d would never leave him. This wasn't the first time he wrestled with the Angel of Death, but it might be his last.

It finally happened, and he had a stroke. The faithful rabbi sat with him in his hospital room, and the sad man became a sorry sight. Weak and intubated, gasping for breath, he made the noticeable sounds of a soul struggling between two worlds—this was the way he felt on most days with his decisions of choosing good and bad.

His kids, conflicted and upset, threw in the towel and stayed away from him. They got busy with their own lives and hoped that one day their dad would be a real father to them, but grudgingly admitted this probably would never be. His love for his addiction became more valuable to him than they were.

His wife, so loyal and good-hearted, always willing to sacrifice herself, and filled with the love of life, was also forced to move away. She tried to help him and set him straight, but to no avail. Reluctantly but faithfully, she came back to sit by his bed once more.

The kids, now grown people of the world, but in their relationship with this man stood in their own island of grief, came for one last visit. Still feeling bitter, angry, and hurt by his drunken actions, they decided to favor their father's request and sit one last time by his bed.

His loving wife, his faithful kids, and his loyal rabbi all waited quietly by his bedside, one last time. Would he wake up? Would G-d perform one more miracle for this old man?

His soon-to-be widow came knocking on my door. She was an old friend and a special woman who saw diamonds where broken stones once were, but she too had had enough.

We sat down like we used to over coffee and a few stories about our lives. My kids were playing on the hardwood floor, and she and I were reminiscing about the days when we used to cook together for Shabbos.

Now, she had moved away to clear her mind from a marriage that just couldn't be fixed, no matter what the effort. Marriage needs two people to make it work, but with his loyalty to his addiction, her hard work became forgotten, and their marriage fell apart.

After much chitchat, she looked up and said, "He was my life, my love, my everything." A silence took over our once loud table, and just the kids' noise could be heard.

I cleared my throat, trying with much difficulty not to show how emotionally pained I felt for my friend. I slid my hand across the table and held her hand tightly. I had hoped that I hadn't overstepped my bounds of a *rebbetzin* to her *congregant*, but to me, she was also such a close, old, dear friend, and the *Yiddishe* mama (Jewish mother) within me just had to reach out to her.

I let a few tears slide down my cheeks, but the rest were shooed away as I replied, "I know, and you did everything that you could for your marriage." We sat there in silence, but I sensed she felt some comfort in her world of pain and confusion.

"Such a sincere, wonderful, and faithful woman," I thought. If only this dying old drunkard would love his family more than he loves and wants alcohol. We got up, whispered our goodbyes, and promised to stay in touch like we always had as I gently closed the door.

Alone in a small room in the rabbi's house sat his little son, a little boy who still believed that all tales have happy endings. My little boy then said to me, "Tatty and you seem so sad about a Jewish man about to die alone. Mommy, I will *daven* for Tatty's friend, for no one deserves to die alone." He took his *siddur* and each day prayed an extra prayer for him. I thought it couldn't hurt, but this old man had run out of favors, or had he?

It happened one day, as my little son was praying, that the phone rang with good news. It was a miracle, and the Jewish man awoke to his family beside him in his hospital room. My little boy sat there stunned. Wow! *davening* (praying) hard really helps: a miracle happened for the old, forgotten man.

He was not forgotten by his Creator, the loyal rabbi, or the rabbi's little son. Friends, family, and those who wanted to say one last goodbye were given a chance.

His chances of survival were slim: his organs were failing, but dying alone should be no one's terrible fate. Prayer, even from a little boy, can help persuade Hashem to give someone one last chance. This time around, he found comfort in talking to his friends and family. Whether his love was shown outwardly or not, a sincere goodbye was deeply felt on both sides.

It was a very emotional moment for each of us who witnessed this special time in which G-d carried him and breathed new life into him. I thought that this was the end of his story.

A few days of proper goodbyes were gifted to him. Still, something unforgettable happened, something that doesn't fit the realm of this world, something that only happens once in a while when Hashem permits Himself to peek through His curtain of miracles within our lives.

This man—who wrestled with the Angel of Death and begged G-d for one more chance to do it right—then had a complete recovery. My little boy still asks me, "Mommy, did my prayers help save that old man's life?"

I always tell him that I definitely think they helped. This Jewish man made a complete recovery and decided to turn his life around. It then became his custom to repay this good rabbi for his kindness. Shabbos morning *minyan* (ten men) is a small token of his gratitude showing where he cares to be, and my little son loves to shake his hand and tell him, "Good Shabbos!"

my fate of staying home

One must allow G-d inside one's life and wait for His plan of Divine providence to be revealed—for that is real living.

"staying home." The term usually brings up the idea of giving up on something, or perhaps one is just too sick to take a step outside. We hear the words "staying home," pause, then move on to our own little things that we busy ourselves with during our day, but someone is staying home, and someone is being left behind.

Some want to go out, to be there to lift up their friend, neighbor, or even a perfect stranger, but their bodies refuse to cooperate, and their minds feel grieved inside. That moment is not just a moment: one feels that their precious time is lost when one stays behind.

What is a real, true moment, one may wonder or ask. It helps make a significant difference, a change, and a way to bring goodness into one's life. The one who loves to give feels overwhelmed when they need to stay home.

My hands felt tied, and knowing that I couldn't be there then forced the mess of feathers seeping out of my overwhelmed bag to burst forth on my floor. A feeling of helplessness and knowing that perhaps I was less important gave way to doubling down on my focus and remembering that Hashem (G-d) is in charge. What G-d thinks is the only thing that really matters, and my feelings and character matter to Him even more than to me.

We drove in two hours before *licht benching* (candle lighting) with the family to get ready for Shabbos. We had just come back from camp after a long journey—but the real journey had just begun. The race to the finish line was just beginning: Shabbos shirts, pants, shoes, and the rest. It was a chase to the end of a good week before Shabbos came walking through the door.

That meant that every little last bit of energy was used for the family. As I finally lit the Shabbos candles, bringing peace into the house, I felt how the day's activities had taken their toll on me.

Just beginning my ninth month and not wanting to let anybody down, I felt this Shabbos was special for important guests. A family was coming that we knew for over a decade; they were special to us, friends that we knew from the beginning of our stay here.

They drove over nine hours to see us, and I felt horrible to witness the bad results. It was pointless for me to go, my limbs weren't cooperating, and I gave into my fate of staying home. I felt self-pity. Of all days, times, and moments—to lose such a precious encounter. What might they be thinking? How could I really explain to them it wasn't my choice?

Choices, choices, choices...they are only part of one side of the equation; the rest is in G-d's hands. His involvement some call fate, but we call it Divine intervention.

What plan did Hashem have in store for me? What trick was up His sleeve to make my head dance to its own story of worry? Whatever His plan, I just had no choice but to see it through to the end.

Sometimes, we must be humble and truly allow G-d to take the reins. This means worrying less and forcing ourselves to remind each other that He is the ultimate decision-maker. Although no one wants to sit and just watch one's life play itself out, sometimes we must take the passenger seat and follow what G-d has planned.

Shabbos morning, I tidied up extra and reminded my husband to please ask this family to come for the afternoon. Holding my breath, I then waited a few more hours until my answer would come. The kids and the family came into my home in their pretty Shabbos attire, followed by the rabbi, dressed all in black in his Chassidic garb.

I thought to myself; it must be a sight to be seen in our little neighborhood. Although I'm sure our neighbors have gotten used to seeing us on the streets looking the way we do, it probably creates waves of bewilderment that make their heads turn.

I finally got my answer after hours of waiting. We said our hellos, and my cheeks hurt so much from smiling; it was such a superb moment. Perhaps even more special was that we had the chance to have just our two families spending precious moments together.

My mind's dance with worry, the holding of my breath, and the nerves to wait and see what G-d had in store were well worth it. It was difficult for me at the time, and my patience for what would come to fruition was long gone. However, Hashem always does come and give a person His grand tour of Divine providence, and for me it was the beautiful Shabbos experience with this family.

G-d is always the master of His paintings, and the little details come into focus at the end. Perhaps the little, minute details are what make the painting that much more exquisite.

The scenery outside was beautiful, for the sun was beginning to set, and it was a happy, picturesque moment. The kids raced up and down the slide, and soon afterward, the swings were flying with happy squeals of delight.

We, worried parents, ran around to each little silly problem we thought was a real concern. Perhaps someone might fall or not have a turn. Finally, it was time to say goodbye until next time. The door slowly closed, my kids tidied up the games, and a beautiful, peaceful, memorable Shabbos came to an end.

My fate of staying home seemed to have been a good one, and the worry of disappointing a friend seemed to have missed its mark. So it seems like another graceful moment is counted, thanked for, and treasured.

a summer experience

Words have power, even in a fun-filled atmosphere.

each summer when we came to my in-laws for camp, one would hear the birds' chirping and the screeching of locusts play cat and mouse around their little game of routine attention of who can scream the loudest in an already busy home. Perhaps they too felt left out. The slamming of doors can be loudly heard, and it's the shouting of many little voices that capture the hearts of their loving grandparents.

We quickly enter the perfectly tidied house and gently rest our bags on the carpeted floor. There's nothing like the feel of home and enjoying the smells of the traditional old recipes.

The noisemakers in a grandmother's kitchen start with boiling pots and pans that blow loud whistles onto the little stovetop. Soon the hugs and laughter will subside, and the caregivers will prepare the family to be one step ahead of the chaos for the hectic, fun-filled summer.

I remember when my oldest son was ready to go to camp. It was a day full of the mixed emotions of elation and sadness. This great feeling of my son becoming more of a little person battled against my worries that he would acquire some kind of independence.

In fact, it could be considered giving him the greatest of gifts: a voice of his own, a way to experience memories shared with friends, all perfectly expressed in a fun-filled Jewish atmosphere.

The classroom was lit with shiny faces of a welcoming spirit. There were toys placed perfectly in each space that the eye would touch, and he was privileged to have lots of the special building blocks of his preference.

I remember how he clasped my hand so tightly, not wanting to let go of me even for a hairbreadth of time. There were tears of fear in his little, clear blue eyes. "Mommy, please, don't leave me!"

The feeling of heartbreak washed over me as I stared at my little mini-me. I felt I must be stronger than allowing myself to feed his fear. I replied in a quiet but firm voice, "Mommy said it would be alright. Now go play with your friends!"

I heard a familiar laugh as I looked up; it was my mother-in-law laughing so hard that tears came to her eyes.

As we stepped outside of the classroom, she said in a quizzical tone, "Mommy said it would be alright"? From then on, it became the family joke that if anything is going wrong in your life or if you feel upset, the saying that "Mommy said it would be alright" put us all back to where we should be.

As one sits alone at home or work for a brief time, one can become like those empty nesters. It is the unknown that captures the mind of each parent. The heartbreak is in wondering if their child will succeed.

Have we done everything that we can to make them comfortable? Are the stories my kids tell me just to get a reaction from me, or are they their new reality?

It's these emotion-filled little wonderings that can get one into trouble with kids, counselors, staff, and even ourselves. Even the strongest of mothers can be taken down by the silliest and pettiest of nerves.

When a child goes to summer camp, it's the little letters or phone calls that create the rounds of worries that hop from parent to parent. It's the forgotten laughter, songs, and life that camp can only give to our little treasures. The energy becomes lost, and all that remains is the thought that this experience is bothersome to me, him, her, or them.

If there was a chance to place ourselves into the counselors', head counselors', or even the director's minds and to read their thoughts, we would understand how they are trying to bring happiness and well-being to their campers. Unfortunately, the great summer fun passes, and it's replaced with these minute interactions that we base our verdict upon.

Sometimes, our kids can exaggerate and willingly decide to pull the rug from underneath us, just for a little extra attention in the fervent hope of bringing out our mother hen and allow chaos to take over our inner senses and intuition.

The why and how of understanding the clown in the box may never be answered. We find ourselves stuck inside this game of sorts, where the edge of the seat becomes our new luxury. It's the tireless waiting that haunts you at each turn until you receive the letter, phone call, or smile that lets you know that you can now breathe again.

However, one is taught that the musing of children should always be carefully placed into thirds. One should never take their words at face value and should take their worries and complains down many notches. After every single day of worry and heartache, it becomes our anticipated wait for the children to exit those big camp doors and fly into our arms.

It becomes our excitement to eagerly greet them and hug them for all eternity, holding our breath in hopes that the day was perfect, and forgetting for a split second that tomorrow we will do it all over again.

the wedge who ruined a family

Putting the real effort in is very helpful in one's life.

an artful friend, and one who seems heartless in her endeavors, takes revenge on another. "Am I really so deserving of all these tricks and hurtful gossip?" the man says out loud, but there's no reply because he is alone.

A man stands broken in the doorway, waiting to be told it is not true. The door stands wide open; it brings a coldness, a hard truth from the Frozen Tundra.

The coldness enveloped the warm indoors until all the warmth seemed to disappear. The man realized that he had just lost his family; all he ever cared about is gone—and without even a goodbye.

He barely whispers to himself the truth of what his new reality is and what he tried so hard to make. He wanted the family to succeed in staying together, but it was hopeless. He remembered that at every turn, and he kept trying to restart his efforts to repair his marriage, but he felt things were sliding and did not know what to do.

"The problem—is it really me?" he wonders. After working so hard to overcome the many obstacles that he faced, can it really be that life is so cruel, and that one spouse would take revenge on another permanently?

It is a cold winter, and the man walks into his home. It was filled with empty places where his family should be, and regret was written all over the walls. The door is left open; his wife is gone, and the children have vanished into thin air!

His heart is beating fast: "How long have they been gone?" Yet, he remembers that this is not the first time his wife ran away. He wonders aloud to himself, "Is it the last?"

He decided that getting busy being proactive was best course to take, and many phone calls were made until an answer was finally given. The answer was not very good, and the hard truth was revealed: his wife and family ran away and wouldn't be coming back this time.

As the phone kept ringing, people demanded that he give divorce papers, and he needed to do it immediately! He couldn't believe that this would be the end of his sad story. He could barely understand what had happened. It was no use: the court would favor her and her story, for she was conniving, and she was the mother.

It is more complicated to be a single father in divorce, and how would he be able to prove that he was a good father? It is usually "he said, she said," but could he at least try, for his children's sake? Could he try to bring them back into his life, even if he might not win?

As each day seemed longer and lonelier, this sad young man remembered how it all started: the laughs, the disagreements, and the different views on life. Why did he settle with her? He knew he was not perfect and needed everything a certain way, but why did everything have to be a fight?

He remembered every week sitting down with the rabbi for family counseling sessions and *Shabbos* night dinners. They were hard times but good times; his kids were happy, and he and his wife felt at peace too.

The family counseling was hard and difficult—another checklist of what to do—but it was too difficult to examine oneself for real. Neither he nor his wife really wanted change, and now a shattered family is the remnants of his dream.

His wife spent many difficult moments in my kitchen discussing her hardships. It helped for the long week until Shabbos, but most of the time nothing I said helped at all. Our friendship was cherished on my side, and on a day that she especially appreciated our friendship, it was on her side too.

However, most of the time, the effort was only on my side; she put in effort only when she needed me, but that too is the life of *shluchim*.

We are there for each person in need, and sometimes our effort and affection are a lonely road when no effort is felt from the other side.

The father and husband, still in a lot of emotional pain, reminisces with us about his painful regrets and emotions that are bursting inside him as tears fall down his cheeks.

He remembered that a few months earlier his wife had left him just as suddenly and gone to a friend's house. She wanted him to beg her to come back home. Well, that seemed petty at the time, and something he felt that he should never do.

Eventually, she brought the kids home, and life became a bit nicer as both of them tried to make things work out. They became comfortable in their newfound friendship with one another and decided to not continue coming to my husband and me for help.

Those long weeks, which felt like an eternity for my husband and me, didn't seem so long for them, and they both let their guard down on working on themselves—and their marriage.

It seemed to happen quickly that they moved a bit further away to spend more *Shabbosim* by themselves. It came to them slowly, this feeling of their making a mistake by not continuing to seek help and guidance.

Their few young Jewish neighbors also didn't seem to help them with their unfortunate tragedy in which this family was spiraling out of control.

This time a tricky friend helped to convince her, the wife, that the problem was all this man's fault, and freedom from marriage was the real dream that she should be chasing. The tickets were ordered, and not even a goodbye was said. The tricky friend who always seemed so nice, but way too nosy, had succeeded in creating a broken family.

The problems in their marriage were real, and both parties were to be blamed, but the friend never saw it that way and became the wedge. She came between this young, embattled couple; therefore, the real problem could not be fixed. Each little, big, and ugly fight kept piling up until it came crashing down on them on all sides, and there was no fixing the flooded house.

"Perhaps," I wondered to myself, feeling grief and shock at the outcome of what I thought would somehow work out in the end, "is the tricky friend really him and her? Is that the real wedge between the couple, when they chose to not look at the situation to fix it but to remain on each side of their fence?" It seemed to me that they became a tricky friend to one another, and now both were alone, and the family was broken.

I felt so sad knowing that so many hours and lost time was put into making their children into better people, and now only she will raise them. The extra shopping partner, the little smiles and hugs, the hours of education and love put in are slowly fading as just a memory— a memory their children will forget, but as they get older they'll wish to hold onto those good moments of the past.

The competition between the two of them is over, and there is no real victor, for a broken home never sprouts any true winners. This is what losing really feels like, and the game between them is over.

We all lost: the couple, the children, and my husband and me. We all became the losers. It turns out we cannot change anyone unless they want to change for real. The only ones we can really change are ourselves, and that is where real change grows and begins.

the nudnik

The nudnik knows her job,
but one must remember theirs as well.

the *shluchim* bid farewell to Crown Heights' comforts and chose to be faithful shepherds to every corner of a forgotten town. Our hearts beat with excitement, and we invested ourselves with all kinds of people, lost stones of the earth.

I feel that each person deserves to be cared for and looked after, no matter what the circumstance. Our job, as the rabbi and *rebbetzin* of a community, is to channel each person into developing themselves better. If they need something, we are always there and come running regardless of if we are called or not.

It then happens that this dedication in which we serve our community crochets each person into part of a unit. This brings distant individuals who are not used to merging into a whole unit as a Jewish community.

We, their safety net and spiritual parents, become like dedicated grandparents hovering over a brand-new baby. We proudly guard them, our treasure stores, for all hours of the day and night.

We feel that the more we give to people, the more people will appreciate our effort and only ask for possessions in an actual time of need. Unfortunately, that isn't always the case, for there is always a *nudnik* in the community—a person who bothers you only for the sake of bothering.

I remember hearing about a woman who truly and with the utmost sincerity had found her heritage and reconnected to her Judaism.

When we as emissaries hear this *ma'aseh* (story), it changes the beat in our pulse, and our souls feel full of gold.

This sincere tale creates a few moments of colorful bubbles that float above us, and then as fast and as colorful as they fly, they sink. It was then that she, the nudnik, was discovered.

That moment, that discovery of circular bliss comes spiraling down to the ground. The nudnik's passion to be burdensome sucks all the energy out of the air, and like a desperate gravitational pull, our positive hope is dragged to the earth as a leaded weight.

True intentions became a thing of the past, and in her game, we were introduced as her pawns. It happened when she, with incredible vigor, started sending letters, letters of great penmanship at all hours of the night. Since we never want to leave one with a question, the answers came as the ink lay fresh on the screen.

The emails usually were long and full of tedious questions, obvious questions, and questions just to ask, to let you know that they were there. I was extremely naive about this type of attitude and felt burdened by this guiltless intrusion.

When we meet people, we try to always get to the big picture. Who are your parents? Where did you grow up? What school did you go to? These intrusive questions bother all of us. Why do you need to know this, is always our first thought, but what happens when we really need to know these types of answers?

After years of responding to all of her empty letters full of mischievous penmanship, other mysterious happenings started taking place in our Chabad house. It became clear that she was one who abhorred the idea of borders and misconstrued the line between what's right and what's wrong.

It doesn't end with just us; she started tormenting others, and her games became too noticeable to allow them to continue. After much persuasion, she reluctantly went to a therapist.

We were waiting fervently to hear the diagnosis in hopes of this being a medical condition, but to our total dismay, we found out that there was nothing really wrong with her and that this behavior is just who she was!

The mind games that she played and replayed with us were her own creativity; it was a devastating blow, after years of working with a person, to then find out you've been played.

The nudnik is the one who finds comfortable ground and harbors a rooted pride in taking complete advantage of humankind. It becomes a business she treasures and a top priority to become bothersome. Throughout this tough ordeal, we were true to ourselves. Our manner and demeanor to her were polite, kind, and respectful.

So, we held a short talk to discuss the outcome of a master game player. As the discussion with her began, her words were chosen to be full of excuses filled with endless threats. We contrasted and chose light, and our words were of truth and full of care. We painfully announced that she was not welcome unless things changed.

Our community was smaller than most, and like in all small communities, news spreads fast. This had a terrible impact! She was quick, fast, and in a hurry to tell everyone about the rabbi and his wife.

She now actually had a real game to play, compared to her millions of other little ones. Whereas before, we were able to dissipate those easily, now it seemed this specialty had wings of its own.

This craft of hers was much too personal and a true hardship to a good teacher's soul. Our response was to be silent and polite even though it was like a spear that tore into our hearts.

However, for our community, the fireworks died down within a month, and then like usual, life moved on for the *shluchim*. Somehow, even after all of it, we are more than ever wanting to put in the extra-long hours to help those in need, even when someone might take things hard.

The lesson I learned from this story was through our response. We choose, as the couple who raised a community, to be silent and not make a *shturem* (storm) as she did. People notice everything, even when there is just silence. It became our reaction to different situations that truly count.

In this way, we lead others by example by showing the community how to react to negative behavior. It isn't always easy to be silent or do what's right. At the end of the day, it's between you and G-d. You must ask yourself, "Did I do all that I can to be a better person? What are my motivations for this response?"

If the realization is that it's from a place of love and care and that others need to be kept safe, then that's the right decision. After everything is said and done, one must let Hashem (G-d) do His part.

the cradle
before the baby

A seventh son is beloved.

after a sleepless night, our beautiful son was alright and ready to enter his special day, his day of circumcision. Why does it always seem like that the fathers are happy and calm, while the mothers are nervous and weeping?

After six boys, I wondered if my seventh son really needed my sweat, nerves, and tears. It's for the same routine, the same *mohel*, and the same covenant with G-d.

Yet, like clockwork, the pacing and nerves before each *bris* (circumcision) began. I looked at the cradle before the baby was summoned to be an important guest at his special party. The grand occasion was done in the open, but it felt like behind closed doors for the one who's the mother.

My mind told me this is what I spent many nights waiting for—my son to join us. But instead, my heart thought of the unknown moment that a single cry would consume my whole being.

The time went quickly with *l'chaim* (to life) and *mazal tov* (congratulations) for a baby who now joined the team as one of the men. The baby was sound asleep, and some wine would soothe his discomfort as I, holding my treasure, began readying myself to serve my son of all his little needs.

As we were getting ready for this special day, our seventh son finally had his circumcision. It felt inspiring for the seventh time, the seventh son, and our community was more eager than ever to greet us.

People from every place and every angle were going up the ramp to our Chabad house to say their hellos and *mazal tovs* (congratulations). The shouts of the seventh boy were heard, and many eager, smiling faces took their seats in anticipation.

My mind somehow must have forgotten, and in all the worry, care, and hurry, our big family added the *simchah* (joyous occasion) of a seventh son, and its meaning was left behind with the crumbs in the corner.

Like all my boys before, my youngest son was born with jaundice; extra care and time was needed. It was a hard beginning for us as a family. Yet it was one that we got used to with each miracle boy born to us. It was full of sleepless nights and making sure that he ate well. Then the bilirubin lights were encircled around him, which insured that the yellow would disappear.

The party for the *bris* was just getting started, and instead of feeling overwhelmed, the work was done before I could lift a finger. The rabbi himself had already prepared the food and ambiance. He was a silent partner who begged to remain hidden behind the curtains, but his work was noticed, and the entrees were perfect; the room was set beautifully, and although I knew it would be, it caught me by surprise.

My eyes circled the perfect room, wondering to myself how, in the middle of the Frozen Tundra, it could be so perfect. I then went downstairs to prepare, and the ladies followed me down by my side.

The guests were people of all different circumstances; some of their faces had been absent for a while, some were from our regular crowd-like family, and others were new. Even surprise guests, who were themselves emissaries, made a real effort to come, making it feel so much more special.

There was a special guest: a little, old, but holy man, with his nice smile and over fifty years at his post. He always seemed to create a joyous occasion on his own with his hard efforts to come as the star in an already brightly lit sky.

My helpers carefully plated the food while I tried to work slowly and not overdo it; a few ladies came and shockingly exclaimed that I looked like I didn't just have a baby! I was surprised but felt complimented, and

I wondered what a tired, exhausted mother should look like? What were they expecting me to look like?

I'm an emissary first and then a person. I want to—and live to—make others happy and comfortable, and only then do I notice my own needs and wants.

Those who were going to frost the cake flew down the stairs to help me. They were three Jewish women from families that I'd struggled to be in touch with, and it surprised me that they readied themselves to help.

Each one of them was so dedicated, coming with gifts for my *simchah*, which were incredibly appreciated. It was special for me to see them roll up their sleeves, get involved in my *simchah*, and be a part of this special day.

The frustrating chance to ask them to be a part of our Hebrew school was slowly breezing itself away. I was excited and relieved that they were part of our *simchah* and chose to include themselves in our community. I wanted to just live in the moment, but my mind wandered to thoughts of, "should I encourage them to go to Hebrew school?"

What would draw them to come and be a part of it? I realized that sometimes I needed to let things play themselves out and enjoy the time as it was, just letting things be. Rome wasn't built in a day, and neither will the community. It will take time to plant and replant beautiful and exquisite flowers.

A great baker and master of cookies came to watch his masterpiece be handed out. His smile was glued on in its place, and with a short burst of conversation, he added to the excitement of the *simchah*.

The rushed but laid-back feel of all the helpers in my kitchen was a great moment. So many hands were being productive and moved with alacrity and precision.

I then reluctantly went upstairs with lots of persuasions because I didn't want to see the prep. I handed my littlest son to the *kvateren* (the couple who carry the baby at the circumcision), and it was to a most special couple that was privileged to be blessed with this honor on this day.

Finally, I heard the loud cry and *mazal tov*; my son was then given a great name for his already loud personality. The *mohel* (the circumciser) soon came, holding the baby. As I listened to his precise instructions of what to do, my extreme discomfort became obvious to me, let alone others in the room, with my new added role. I now needed to be his nurse and keep my son safe to heal properly.

I got up to leave the small room that was way too small for four adults to function so carefully and to stay so focused. Then to my surprise, I was stuck in the little room by myself to watch a *Minchah minyan* (afternoon prayer service) of men come together for prayer.

The big room blocked me from entering, and I wondered why I was meant to witness this particular service. I had no idea why but felt that maybe it was to hear my eldest son say amen so emphatically, or to hear and watch my husband pray with such love to his Creator. No one knows the real reasons for Divine providence.

The laws of modesty kept ringing in my head, and I waited for the *minyan* to end. I carefully and slowly made my way upstairs when the master baker of cookies stopped me and said, "It was such a privilege to be a part of such a great *simchah*."

Those words coming from him were shocking and uplifting at the same time. I wondered how such kind words could change the room's mood and make it look less serious and more jubilant.

I started saying my goodbyes and was trying to get all my kids in one place simultaneously, but my struggle became obvious to all the eyes in the room. They were glued to me as if I was leading a circus with baby gorillas on the loose.

After promising all kinds of special treats, the kids were ready to behave. I then heard an almost whisper that came from an old, familiar face. This kind man had a history with us: he was a man with a vision and someone I truly respected, and even more than that, revered.

He then said a bit less quietly that he was sorry he sat at the *minyan*, and it was because he had double leg surgery. I couldn't believe he drove all this way and went up and down the stairs—after leg surgery!

The icing on the cake for me was his embarrassment. He did not stand up and was worried that I got the wrong impression.

I guess I always felt comfortable speaking my mind and told him that I was grateful he came. I continued emphatically that I was even more thankful he came after double leg surgery to be at our *simchah*.

As he left, the impression of his commitment embraced my mind and hugged my thoughts as I slowly walked down the driveway with my children on all corners of me.

reopening during a pandemic

The gate of mercy was open, and we pushed through many doors on this day.

OUr Chabad house is a place for each person in need to come and stay and a place that never turned a soul away. No matter who the person was, no matter what the hour, no matter what the discomfort, we tried to make every effort to be there and ease their burden.

Our energy comes from seeing happy faces and happy stories, but this time life was different. As spiritual parents, we had to stay closed and form a united front to protect our community from this coronavirus.

Each day it felt like we were sitting in a dark waiting room, waiting eagerly to be called, but we never were. Then came the hurricane of the night, and its worrisome wait was highlighted even more than the day. We came to the startling realization that this was our new reality, and it could even take years of living in a limbo-like state before it was all over.

Could we survive this as a family? As a community? As a nation? All I had were hazy questions and no good answers, not even to comfort myself regarding the what-could-be.

It was late at night, and finally, all the boys were sleeping; the house sparkled, and my husband was finally home. As usual, we started our weekly meeting, catching up on which direction or particular thing needed our focus.

My husband placed a surreal surprise in my lap, saying that this week should be the week. It was a brave decision, but one that he felt was right. He wanted to open up the Chabad house, and would I please consider it. He had out-of-towners in desperate need of a place to stay, and it was the right time, or so he felt, to open up overall.

I was shocked, hesitant, and then decided that it was in our best interests that a very certain "no" had to be proclaimed. "No? How can I tell people no? They have no food for Shabbos and will have nowhere to stay. The hotel is way too expensive for all six boys," my husband said desperately, both to himself and to me at the same time, looking to find answers to voice our own personal questions of why during what felt like an Egyptian plague.

Trying to find my voice in a world that toppled itself over, trying to find a real answer to a real question filtering out a rabbi's overprotective stance, I agreed with him emotionally. Still, logically, I knew as he did that our place was closed, and our hands were cuffed.

I had to refocus us, which felt strange to me, because my many ideas were normally being filtered out daily by a very logical and good-head-on-his-shoulders type of rabbi. I, and not my husband, had to be the one to say no—and give a good reason besides the obvious.

"Look, they will be sleeping on a cold floor with only sleeping bags to keep them warm. That part of our building is not quite finished, and the floor needs to be replaced. Besides, it's late in the week, already Wednesday night. We will have to figure this out with our fellow brotherhood and sisterhood of *shluchim* before opening," I said, spewing out explanations knowing that nothing would appease the rabbi in his desire to help a fellow in need.

"Then hours and hours will be spent cooking, cleaning, and rearranging for them to stay in a safe and protected way. It seems like there is no way this is going to work. Am I wrong?"

Then my husband said with one last effort and feeling the worry for those out-of-town *bochurim* (boys that go to rabbinical school). "There is no choice! The hotel will be hundreds of dollars, and the *bochurim* (boys that go to rabbinical school) did not bring enough money with them, so we have to help them!"

"I'm sorry, but we cannot," I said in almost a whisper because it was such a hard and sad thing to say this little but strong word "no."

I wrestled with this word, this word that held so much power in such a difficult time that I felt myself crawl inside the word "no," but outside the conversation for a brief moment to collect my thoughts. I sat there and continued drinking my tea, and we slowly finished our meeting.

The next day I started preparing Shabbos for my family only, like I always did during this time of social distancing. My husband came flying into the house with such a big smile that I had to ask what happened. Our brotherhood and sisterhood of *shluchim* felt that most places were opening up, and they decided that opening our place in our location was a good idea.

"Wow!" I got excited for a minute and felt like I had my wings back, but then I controlled my happiness, worried about the fall later on if I got too excited, only then to be told it was a joke. "Are you joking with me? How is it possible?"

One of those scarce moments that I can look at his phone or he can look at mine happened. We protect our congregants and believe that words of privacy can only be broken in emergencies, even amongst one another. His phone was open and there it was: they all agreed our Chabad house could be reopened. We knew that we didn't really need their OK, but it felt good to have their blessing and emotional support.

It felt so strange to think that we could be free when our wings had been clipped for four long months. We became painfully aware that we were caged from all humanity and all of our responsibilities. It was a scar that would take a long while for our community to heal from.

Would we even know how to fly and reach out to others again? Would we even remember how to keep each part that made our Chabad house unique, still special? Can it really be so balanced, the Chabad house programs, prayer service, and people fitting perfectly like a seesaw flying in mid-air?

The gloom, the despair, the emotional low that all of us felt when we were on lockdown made us feel like we were little ducklings running in circles without their mother, and hoping mother duck would come back and claim us.

It was over! At least to some degree, we were coming out of our restraints. I was on fire, and so was my husband, but our kids' celebration took the crown. Finally, I felt in my element, a bit rusty, a bit shaky, but more than ready to roll up my sleeves and get moving.

I spent many hard hours cooking, cleaning, and focusing every single moment to take this task to the finish line. Another family of out-of-towners was excited about how their Shabbos would be, and through their masks, they announced to us, "Wow! Did you put this all together in less than eight hours?"

What was there to say with sweat dripping off our faces and our masks covering our mouths. She then continued, "And I feel guilty that I'm not helping out." It was interesting that she felt that way, and I realized that usually, most guests do help out when they can, but my excitement for the reopening blind-sided me even to attempt to get stuck on it.

Shabbos was here, and we walked back to the Chabad house to join everyone. A feeling of excitement filled the air, and there was a smell of welcoming as I entered the Chabad house. It was all to be broken with "Mommy, here is your mask." I felt confused for a second because I was stuck in my excitement of finally being back. My little son looked at me again, and in a louder voice, said, "Mommy, you forgot your mask."

I quickly touched my face and realized that I left my mask at home and would have to take the one my son was holding out for me. My elated mood so on fire shriveled up, and I understood that *Moshiach* (the Messiah) wasn't quite here yet and that life would not be the same at all. A place of extreme warmth still held a coolish breeze, and we all looked like scarf-wearing people on a very windy day, or so I told my children to keep their excitement up.

However, my littlest boys loved the masks that they were wearing so much that they chose to make it a competition. Oy! One more worry amongst the calm, I thought to myself. I had to then explain to the little boys that they couldn't wear their masks over their eyes. They finally, and with a real reluctance, decided to listen and allowed their bright pink faces to get some much-needed air.

As I scrubbed the dishes *Motzaei Shabbos* (Saturday night), I realized that it would be a process of adjusting. There were many doors open for us with goodness, positivity, and appreciating the little things that we missed. Yet, at the same time, we were still prisoners of this virus: no hugging, no kissing, and no proximity to anyone but our family. The tables were placed very far apart and guarded; the worried responses were kept very close to our guests.

It's a step up from where we were, and at least we can be spiritual parents to our community again, even if we have to have many rules about being in the same physical room as one another. The saying goes that "this too shall pass," and as one door opens, another door may finally close.

about the author

Esther Feinstein, along with her husband and children, lives in the Midwest and serves as an emissary of the Lubavitcher Rebbe. As one of five thousand couples who aim to transform the world by bringing every individual closer to their Creator, she co-directs a Chabad House—teaching and lecturing, counseling and advising, celebrating and sharing—shaping the community into one extended family.

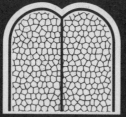

MOSAICA PRESS

BOOK PUBLISHERS

Elegant, Meaningful & Bold

info@MosaicaPress.com
www.MosaicaPress.com

The Mosaica Press team of
acclaimed editors and designers
is attracting some of the most
compelling thinkers and teachers
in the Jewish community today.
Our books are available around
the world.

HARAV YAACOV HABER
RABBI DORON KORNBLUTH